HEROIC STORIES
FROM THE BIBLE

6

Additional materials have been prepared by:
Bob Coffen (word searches)
Sally Dillon (puzzles)
Gerald Wheeler (A Closer Look)

Special biblical and archaeological consultants:
Douglas Clark
Larry Herr
Sakae Kubo
Pedrito Maynard-Reid
Ronald Springett
Warren Trenchard
Douglas Waterhouse

Bible stories by Ruth Redding Brand
Professor Appleby narrative by Charles Mills

Professor Appleby and Maggie B Series
1. *Mysterious Stories From the Bible*
2. *Amazing Stories From the Bible*
3. *Love Stories From the Bible*
4. *Adventure Stories From the Bible*
5. *Miracle Stories From the Bible*
6. *Heroic Stories From the Bible*

To order, call 1-800-765-6955.
Visit us at http://www.rhpa.org

HEROIC STORIES FROM THE BIBLE

6

RUTH REDDING BRAND & CHARLES MILLS

REVIEW AND HERALD® PUBLISHING ASSOCIATION
HAGERSTOWN, MD 21740

The author assumes full responsibility for the accuracy of all facts
and quotations as cited in this book.

Bible texts credited to NRSV are from the New Revised Standard Version of the
Bible, copyright © 1989 by the Division of Christian Education of the National
Council of Churches of Christ in the U.S.A. Used by permission.

Names have been supplied some of the characters in the Bible stories. While
the names reflect those used during the story's particular time period, the
author is not suggesting that anyone in the story was actually so named.

This book was
Edited by Gerald Wheeler
Copyedited by Jocelyn Fay and James Cavil
Designed by Patricia S Wegh
Cover design by Ron J. Pride
Cover illustration by Kim Justinen
Interior illustrations by Joe Van Severen
Typeset: 11/13 Stone Informal

PRINTED IN U.S.A.

02 01 00 99 98   5 4 3 2 1

R&H Cataloging Service
Brand, Ruth Redding
    Heroic stories from the Bible, by Ruth
Redding Brand and Charles Mills

    1. Bible stories.   I. Mills, Charles
Henning, 1950-   . II. Title.   III. Series.

            220.9505

ISBN 0-8280-0968-6

①
Secret Mission

Do you think he heard us?" Maria whispered, her eyes searching the long, high-ceiling room. Pointing at the dark-skinned boy creeping beside her, she added, "Jason made enough noise coming in the window to wake the dead."

"I did not," her companion shot back as he tripped over a metal trash can and tumbled headlong into an umbrella stand.

"Will you guys be quiet!" Stacey breathed between clenched teeth. "My grandfather may be a little forgetful and kinda old, but he's not deaf!"

"Sorry," the boy blushed, picking himself up from the spotlessly polished wooden floor. "That can wasn't there yesterday."

Stacey Roth shook her head from side to side. "We'd never make it as burglars. The only weapon the cops would need to track us down is a good pair of ears. Now if you two will stop running into things and chattering like magpies, we might be able to get this job done before the professor wakes up." She paused. "Besides, we've gotta be back to the main road in five minutes, or Maria's mom will think we fell in a hole or something. So come on!"

The three sixth graders slipped through the early-morning shadows, making their way past rows of glass-covered display cases filled with intriguing objects. Large sturdy tables piled high with carefully arranged and labeled artifacts from around the world rested nearby.

Jason glanced at some of the stone faces staring back at him as he passed—statues carved before the birth of Christ. Brightly woven lengths of cloth, their intricate designs reflecting the skillful workmanship of long-forgotten seamstresses, flowed from tabletops. The warm rays of the rising sun peeking through the windows highlighted their deep textures and soft folds.

Ancient oil lamps, farming tools, and kitchen utensils sat waiting to be admired beside clay tablets covered with strange, mysterious markings.

The paneled walls of the big room supported broad tapestries flaunting battle scenes and visions of unearthly beauty. As many times as Jason and the others had visited this chamber, they'd never grown tired of staring at the puzzling shapes and mystifying objects waiting there.

But today was special, at least it was supposed to be—if they could carry out their secret mission. Silently the three tiptoed into the foyer of the big Victorian mansion and scurried like young phantoms through the kitchen doorway, trying their best not to make a sound.

Wordlessly they circled the breakfast table as each, in turn, took an envelope from their pocket and laid it gently by the shiny toaster. Then, as quietly as they'd come, the children hurried back to the hallway, leaving the three sealed envelopes as the only testament of their presence.

Before long the sound of a door softly closing heralded the fact that the visitors had departed, headed for school and the unknown adventures of a new day.

✗ ✗ ✗

Professor Appleby stared at his reflection in the bathroom mirror. He smiled, then frowned. Tilting his head from side to side, he inspected his face carefully, as if looking for something.

Slowly he stuck out his tongue and moved it back and forth. One eye closed, then the other.

His thin snow-white hair tumbled over his ears like a frozen waterfall. Soft wrinkles ran in random courses about his eyes and cheeks, giving him the appearance, in this particular light, of a very mature and uncommonly pale prune.

"Still got my own teeth," he said out loud, a broad smile filtering his words. "Not too many men my age can say that."

The old man lifted a finger and rubbed it against the bright-white row of upper incisors protruding from under his equally milky mustache. He heard a squeaking sound. "Strong as the day they grew in when I was just a lad," he boasted to himself, his smile broadening. "A thousand years from now, if the Lord doesn't come, they'll open my casket and find my teeth grinning right up at them. No hair, no bones, just a perfect set of molars."

Professor Appleby smacked his lips, frowning at the musty

taste in his mouth. "Better brush 'em," he said. "Good, solid teeth mean a lot to a man, especially on his birthday." He paused. "This is my birthday, isn't it?"

The mansion's sole occupant hurried out into the hallway and stumbled to his bedroom. He grabbed a colorful card resting on the nightstand and read the words scrawled across it in familiar handwriting. "Happy Birthday, big brother," the card announced. "Hope you have a wonderful day. I miss you. Wish I could be there to help you celebrate. But I'm sure Stacey and her friends are planning something exciting just for you.

"Welcome today's visitors to our museum for me. Tell 'em I'm busy looking for more treasures to send. Stay well and remember your sister loves you very much. Hugs and kisses, Maggie B."

The professor pressed the card close to his heart. "I love you too, Maggie," he whispered. "It's been so long since your last visit. When are you coming back again?" He walked to the window, the card still held against his chest. "Stacey's growing up so fast," he said quietly. "And the children—oh, how they love to hear your stories! They're even playing your tapes on the local Christian radio station now. The whole town tunes in each afternoon at 4:30 sharp."

Professor Appleby sat down on the foot of his bed and smiled over at a photograph resting on his dresser. The framed image showed a woman sitting astride a donkey in front of blowing tent flaps. She was wearing the dark, drab garb of the desert Bedouin, a nomadic tribe of wanderers who call the hot sands of the Middle East home. Peeking from behind loose strands of pure white hair were a pair of loving blue eyes. The face was deeply lined but glowed with health and vigor. The grin was proud, eager, happy.

"They're building a new museum just for you at the community college," the old man said to the picture. "I wrote all about it in my last letter. You should get it soon, if the postal service can track you down."

He lifted the handwritten message. "Thanks for the card, Maggie. You always remember my birthday. Always." His voice faded as his shoulders sagged slightly. "Don't know how many more I'll have. Not as young as I used to be." The man shook his head.

"Listen to me, carrying on like some elderly codger on his deathbed. Why, I've got a bunch more years on my account. You'll see. Just hope I last as long as my teeth."

That said, the man jumped up and hurried from the room. He'd continue his conversation with Maggie B later. For now, he had things to do and people to meet. In less than an hour Professor Appleby's Museum of Really Old Stuff—as the children had lovingly named his home-based gallery—would be open to the public. He wanted to be ready when the first guest arrived, eager to see what life was like before Christ walked the dusty paths of planet earth.

Soon oatmeal bubbled on the stove as Professor Appleby wandered about the kitchen preparing his breakfast. He hadn't bothered to glance at the table until he was reaching down to plop two fresh slices of wheat bread in the toaster.

"What's this?" he gasped, seeing the three small envelopes resting on the very spot his spoon and fork usually occupied. "Did I forget to mail some letters yesterday?"

The man picked up the mysterious objects and turned them over slowly. Each was addressed to "Professor Appleby, the neatest, most wonderful old man in the world and best friend to children everywhere."

"Well, well," he chuckled. "Maybe somebody else remembered my birthday, and I'll bet their names are Stacey, Maria, and Jason." Slitting open the envelopes, he read the words written on the enclosed cards.

Maria's message was short and to the point, a perfect reflection of the little Mexican girl who'd written it. "Good morning, Professor. Happy Birthday. Your big gift will arrive someday soon, I hope. Love Maria."

The old man smiled. "Gift, huh? Can't get too many of them in this life. Always room for one more."

The next message was from Jason, the more "artistically inclined" member of the group, as the professor enjoyed referring to the young, energetic African-American with a heart of pure gold. The boy's words were in the form of a rap poem. As the professor began reading, the rhythm of the text started his body swaying and toes tapping.

"The sun comes up on a brand-new day
   "You're another year older, so what do I say?
"Happy Birthday, Professor, what a hap-py sound
   "As you blow out your candles, and you look all around
"At your friends and fam'ly saying, 'How do you do?'
   "Hope your joys are many and your trou-bles few.
"Mister Ap-ple-by, this is all I'll say.
   "Your gift will be comin' on another day.
"So relax and chill, try to have some fun,
   "And al-ways remember that you're NUMBER ONE!"

By the end of the reading Professor Appleby was swaying and bobbing around the table like a spastic juggler.

Stacey's card was hand-printed like the rest, and contained paintings of flowers and flying birds. In carefully crafted letters she'd written, "Dear Grandpa, It's your birthday (like you didn't know that already), and we (Maria, Jason, and I) want to give you a surprise party (except it can't be a surprise, because we decided we're not very good at keeping secrets and you'd fig-ure out what we were up to by just looking at us, so we're going to give you a regular party and you can look surprised if you want to).

"Don't fix yourself any supper. Mom and the rest of us will be over tonight at 6:00 with a really neat cake that I and Maria are going to bake (Jason said he'll decorate it with pictures of fruit and stuff) and some ice cream (chocolate, your favorite), as well as some pizza.

"Mom said we should invite Miss Baker from the community college, since she thinks you're an interesting old man. So have a nice day, and we'll see you tonight.

"Love you bunches and bunches, Stacey.

"PS: We're going to give you some gifts (nothing expensive, because we're just kids and aren't rich). BUT a special surprise is coming and won't be ready for a while. (I don't know if I can wait that long. Guess I'll have to—as you know, I hate waiting for any-thing!) See you tonight."

Professor Appleby grinned broadly. "Imagine," he said to himself, "an un-surprise party just for me by my favorite people in all the world. And Miss Baker will be coming too. This puts a whole different slant on the festivities.

"Wonder if I have any of that neat-smelling aftershave lotion Stacey gave me three years ago," the old man mused. "What was that called? Sea Power? Mighty Dog—no, that's a pet food. Oh yes, Wild West. That's it. I'll splash on my Wild West. That should catch Miss Baker's attention. After all, she thinks I'm interesting. Stacey said so."

The old man walked from the room deep in thought. "Wonder if I have time to get a haircut in town. I could do laundry, too. Want to look my best for Stacey and the others." He paused and lifted a finger. "And Miss Baker, of course."

Back in the kitchen the oatmeal slowly bubbled and steamed as two brown pieces of bread popped up from the toaster.

✗ ✗ ✗

Shortly after school let out that afternoon, three excited pre-teens burst into the Roth house on Fern Street and set up an immediate command post in the brightly lit kitchen overlooking the small, carefully clipped back yard. Their mission for the afternoon? Bake the most beautiful birthday cake Valley Springs had ever seen—or tasted.

Stacey and Maria were in charge of the mixing bowl, while Jason set his hand to creating the icing and designing the "look" of the product, as he so professionally labeled his duties.

But no amount of activity could keep the three workers from remembering to switch on the radio to station WPRL at exactly 4:29. That's when, Monday through Friday, Mr. McDonald, the station manager, announced it was "Maggie B Story Time." Today was no exception.

"Good afternoon, boys and girls, ladies and gentlemen," the smiling voice echoed from the little radio/cassette player combination fastened securely under the cabinet near the sink. "We begin a new series of adventures from our much-traveled friend, Maggie B. For the next few weeks we're going to learn about biblical heroes, and personally, I can hardly wait.

"So pump up the volume, grab a fruit drink, make yourself comfortable, and listen as Maggie B begins our first excursion into the past. Her story is called 'Not a Thread or a Sandal Strap.' Enjoy!"

Almost immediately the firm but friendly voice of Professor Appleby's sister filled the room and the imaginations of listeners all around Valley Springs.

✕ ✕ ✕

Lot chewed his lower lip and tried not to show how nervous he felt. The people of Sodom and surrounding cities yelled and cursed. Closing his eyes for a moment, he tried to shut out the memories of the shocking things he had seen them do. These people, it seemed to Lot, had no respect for each other. He had seen wild animals treat each other with more dignity. Whatever they wanted to do, he decided, he had better go along with them.

Now a great brute of a man shouted louder than the rest. "For 12 years our five cities have paid unfair tribute to this foreign king, this Chedorlaomer. Twelve years, I tell you! And for what? For nothing! We get nothing for all the goods we give him! Well, our cities are not going to pay any more! No more tribute!"

The crowd picked up the cry. "No more tribute! No more tribute! No more tribute!"

Lot found himself chanting along with the others, but his stomach felt like a cold knot of fear. He would not admit it, even to his wife, but sometimes he wished he had remained with Abram.

But Lot had reason to be afraid. The revolt against Chedorlaomer was sure to invite his anger. And that anger would mean just one thing—war. The only question was When would it happen?

People in the rebellious cities tried to act brave, but as they went about their daily work, they glanced fearfully over their shoulders. At night they tossed and turned on their mats, their hands never far from their spears or maces.

Then on an ordinary day, out of the hot mists hovering over the Dead Sea with the glaring sun at their backs, the armies of Chedorlaomer arrived. With three other kings and their armies they appeared around a bend in the lush irrigated valley in which Sodom lay. Angrily they marched up to the wooden gates the people of Sodom had hastily closed against them.

The invaders broke through the mud-brick city walls. Sweeping through Sodom with their axes and maces, they slaughtered all who tried to defend themselves, and burned the city to its foundations.

Then the kings of Sodom, Gomorrah, and three other cities banded together with their armies and turned on the attackers, but it was no use. In fear of their lives, the soldiers of Sodom and Gomorrah turned on their heels and ran. Slipping, falling, smashing through bushes and stumbling over rocks, they ran. Where could they hide? Suddenly they remembered the bitumen pits where they mined natural asphalt. Here would be a place Chedorlaomer's men would not find them. The rest of Sodom's soldiers fled to caves in the hills.

Soon all the cities surrendered, and the conquering armies rounded up men, women, and children as prisoners of war. The conquerors helped themselves to all kinds of food and other valuable items. They broke into houses and stole clothing, gold, silver, and jewels. Rushing upon peacefully grazing herds and flocks, they drove the frightened, wild-eyed animals before them in a cloud of dust.

Then as suddenly as they had swept into the rebellious cities, the invaders left. But with them they took captives and all the goods that they had stolen, leaving the cities empty piles of smoking rubble.

Lot and his family stumbled along with the rest of the frightened crowd of captives. What lay ahead of them? they wondered. They knew only that they would be made slaves. For the rest of their lives they would be made to sweat and toil and do anything that their masters commanded.

His wife and children cried. And Lot prayed, not to idols, but to the God of Abram.

☼ ☼ ☼

One morning as Abram and Sarai swallowed the last of their breakfast of barley bread, figs, and yogurt made from goat's milk, a stranger stumbled toward their tent. His clothes were torn and dirty, and dust caked his face. He wheezed from exhaustion and seemed about to faint.

Quickly Abram ran to his side. "Come in, stranger, and rest," he invited as he helped him into his tent and gently laid him down on the carpets and pillows.

Sarai rushed to bring him water and to fix some food for him. When the stranger felt better, he told Abram of the attack

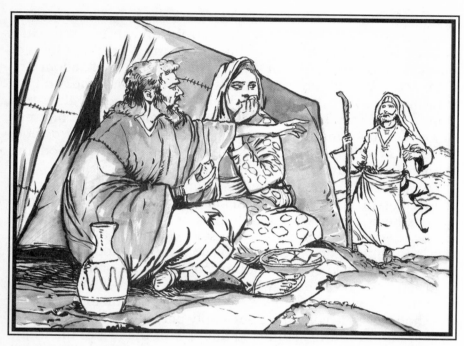

on Sodom, Gomorrah, and the other cities, and of all the people taken captive. He himself had been a captive, but had managed to escape. "And," the stranger said, "your nephew Lot is one of those captives. The attackers took everything he and his family owned."

That was all Abram needed to hear. He loved his nephew, and if Lot was in trouble, he would help him. God had blessed Abram with helpful friends in Hebron, so Abram told them the terrible thing that had happened. The friends had promised each other that if they were ever in trouble, they would help each other. They were eager to keep their word.

Then Abram called his own household together and told them that Lot had been taken captive. Abram's household had many men who had been trained to use weapons in self-defense. Abram chose 318 of them and prepared to attack the armies of Chedorlaomer and the other kings who had captured Lot.

Abram could have reasoned, of course, that Lot deserved whatever happened to him for moving to a city like Sodom. Or he could have just stayed safely in his tent and prayed for Lot. But Lot was a member of Abram's family, and Abram was ready to risk his life for Lot and the other captives. He knew that God would be with him just as He had always been.

"This is the plan," Abram explained to his men. "We will attack at night. They won't be expecting us, and in the dark they won't know that there are only a few of us compared to many of them. We will divide up into three groups and will all attack at the same time. Our goal is to bring back all the captives unharmed. Also we will get back all the stolen goods. Are you ready?"

So on a night black as a raven's wing, while the hopeless captives sat in silence and their captors laughed and bragged, Abram led his troops against their camp. Shouts, cries, the sound of weapon upon weapon, shattered the still night air. Confused and alarmed, the once-triumphant kings and their armies stumbled off into the night. Abram's skilled men made sure they would not come back. They chased them for many days all the way to Hobah, north of Damascus.

Of course all the captives were thankful to Abram and the soldiers. Lot had never before been so glad to see his uncle!

Then someone stepped forward to meet Abram. Melchizedek, the king of Salem (later called Jerusalem), and a priest of the God of Creation, smiled at Abram and offered him bread and wine. The simple offering of common food was Melchizedek's way of saying, "What a fine thing you have done, Abram, in helping people who were in trouble! God is pleased with you."

Then Melchizedek proclaimed God's blessing on Abram. "May God Most High, who made heaven and earth, bless Abram! May God Most High, who gave you victory over your enemies, be praised!"

Abram was thankful to God for being with him. To show God his gratitude, he gave God's priest, Melchizedek, a tenth of all the recaptured goods.

The king of Sodom, hearing reports of Abram's victory, marched north to greet him. "Please keep all the jewels and cattle and herds and silver and gold from Sodom," he said when he arrived. "Just return all the people to their homes. That is all I ask." It was a humble request for a king, but Abram had the right, as the new conqueror and deliverer, to take everything, perhaps even becoming the new king of Sodom himself.

But Abram wanted nothing. He had learned much since his visit to Egypt. Now he would have no king on earth saying that he had made him rich, nor did he want to owe anything to anyone.

"I don't want a thread from your clothes or a sandal strap," he said. "I'll keep only the food which my young men need. However, my friends who risked their lives with me are entitled to whatever they want."

Abram was giving Lot and others, too, a lesson in how to be unselfish. The people of Sodom returned to their homes with their fine clothes, their jewels, their gold, their flocks and herds, and all their goods. That would not have happened if their rescuer had not been a worshiper of the true God, the God of Creation.

Abram risked his life for his nephew and for people he didn't even know. Some people might think that Abram got nothing out of doing such a kind thing. But of all the happy people who returned to their homes, Abram was the happiest of all, because he knew that God was pleased with him. God was, through Abram, blessing the families of the earth round about him.

⚔ ⚔ ⚔

Maria looked up from her mixing bowl. "That was cool. Imagine how scary it would be if some army came roaring into Valley Springs and took us all captive."

Stacey chuckled. "My mom would be there with her tape recorder getting statements from the advancing troops, you can count on that." The girl picked up a batter-encrusted spoon and held it up in front of Jason as if she was trying to interview him. "So tell me, General, why are you taking all the citizens of this fair town captive?"

Jason blinked, then realized what his friend was trying to do. Lifting his chin and striking a commanding pose, he spoke in as deep a voice as he could muster. "Well . . . uh . . . we need slaves for our factories, farm workers for our fields, and someone to get those nasty stains out of our bathtubs." He leaned forward. "You know, the kind that get in between the tiles. I hate those." Lifting his chin again, he added. "And we need people to polish our cars, sweep our floors, and baby-sit our children while we pillage and plunder and stuff like that." He crossed his arms. "Can't have too much in the way of household goods and cold hard cash, you know."

Stacey grinned, warming to their playacting. "So you'd pillage our village and plunder our people for profit?"

"Probably."

The blond-haired girl shook her head in mock disgust. "You are arrogant and evil, a most disturbing member of society."

Modestly Jason spread his hands. "I do my best."

Maria rolled her eyes. "Cut it out, you guys. The next story is about to begin. Mr. McDonald said it's called 'Miracle at the Jordan,' and I don't want to miss one word."

Jason nodded. "Yes. I must get back to my pillaging." With that he stabbed his spoon into the mixture in his bowl and laughed a deep, loathsome laugh.

Stacey grinned while reaching up and twisting the volume knob on the radio just as Maggie B began her next story.

✕ ✕ ✕

Wide-eyed children and openmouthed adults listened to Joshua's every word.

"Get ready, pack your belongings, and spend this night in prayer, for tomorrow you will cross the Jordan! Then you will see the Lord do wonderful things for you."

A thrill of excitement rippled through the crowd. Tomorrow! *Tomorrow!* Just think, after years of wandering, only one brief night lay between them and the Promised Land. Children chattered excitedly. What would it be like living in the new land? Would they live in houses high on a wall as many people in Jericho did? Would the people in the new land be friendly or mean? Just how would their lives change?

But the older people had other questions. "How will we cross the Jordan?" they asked. "It's flooded and dangerous."

And so it was. Under the warm spring sunshine the far-off snows of Mount Hermon had melted, streamed down the mountain, and tumbled into the four main sources of the Jordan. Already swollen from the winter rains, the melted-snow streams poured into the rushing river.

Now the Jordan surged along, overflowing its banks, its brown waters swirling in dangerous whirlpools. The two spies warned Joshua of the danger in trying to move large numbers of people with their vast herds across the flood.

But Joshua only smiled and held up his hand. A light—the same light that had so often bathed Moses' features—lit his deep dark eyes. And when he spoke, his voice carried the same authority.

"The Lord has spoken to me," he announced in a hushed tone. "He will perform great wonders for you. The ark of the covenant," he turned and nodded in the direction of the sanctuary, "will lead us across the waters."

The camp was busy that night as people followed God's directions, packing their few belongings, washing themselves and their clothes. The priests reverently took the sanctuary apart, ready to carry across the Jordan. Then silence fell, as each person, young and old, talked quietly with God.

In the morning they hastily took down their tents and herded all their animals together. Then 12 priests bent over the covered ark of the covenant. Lacing long poles through the golden rings along the sides, they reverently lifted the sacred ark to their shoulders.

"Stand back! Stand back!" Joshua called. "The Lord requires you to keep a distance of a half mile between yourselves and the priests bearing the ark of God."

Turning to the priests, he instructed, "Walk straight into the Jordan. When your feet touch the water, it will pile up as if held by a mighty dam, and you will cross over on dry ground!"

The priests caught their breaths, hardly able to grasp Joshua's words. A miracle was about to happen!

The priests began to walk forward, the ark slightly swaying with each determined step. Far behind them the rest of the huge crowd began to follow. Hundreds of children scampered along, excited, curious, almost overwhelmed by everything that was happening. The Promised Land at last—just beyond the Jordan!

But as they neared the river, their eyes grew wide with amazement. The narrow, winding course of the Jordan had vanished as the water overflowed the banks and spread out like a lake on both sides. Tall grasses poked up through the floodwaters, while palm trees seemed to wade in its current.

But beyond the grasses the Jordan rushed in angry torrents, carrying sticks and branches along at a frightening speed toward the Salt Sea.

The children looked up anxiously into their parents' faces. But mothers and fathers only tightened their lips and pressed onward, their eyes never leaving the ark.

The priests marched ahead, their eyes on the water, a prayer on their lips. The ground became soggy, and soon each footprint filled with water faster than they could lift a foot and put it down again. Then the water seeped over their sandals and rose to their ankles. Still they did not look back or slow their pace.

Another step found them knee-deep in swirling brown water with the current tugging at their robes. One more step and a fierce tremor suddenly shook the ground on which they stood. The roar of the water upstream suddenly ceased. The water downstream flowed onward as before, quickly draining the ground on which they stood.

The crowd stared, transfixed by the sight. "The priests!" they exclaimed. "Look at them! They're standing on dry ground in the middle of the river!"

Joshua's smile was as bright as the sunshine. "Come!" he invited. "Our God has made a road for you in the middle of the flood! Now cross over to the land He has promised!"

The priests stood firmly on the stony riverbed, holding the ark aloft, while miles upstream the flood waters fought uselessly against God's hand.

For hours the Israelites poured across the riverbed. Children and parents, sheep and goats, donkeys and cattle eased down one bank, crossed the riverbed, and climbed up the other side. And everybody, from toddlers to grandparents, felt a rush of happiness as they first stepped onto the land God had promised.

Finally the last bleating lamb scrambled up the western bank. Then Joshua, his face still wreathed in a splendid smile, spoke in ringing tones to the awestruck crowd. "So that we will never forget what the Lord has done for us this day, I have chosen 12 men, each from one of the 12 tribes of Israel, for a special task."

Curiously, the people watched as 12 strong men, feeling proud and honored, returned to the riverbed, where the priests still stood holding the ark. Carefully examining the ground, each selected a large stone and carried it back to the bank, where the people waited.

"Now build an altar!" Joshua directed. Again the people watched as the men solemnly constructed an altar near the bank of the Jordan.

"In years to come," Israel's leader continued in an even stronger voice, "people may ask, 'What is this monument for?' And you can tell them: 'It is to remind us that the Jordan River stopped flowing when the ark of God went across!'"

Finally the tired but happy priests, still balancing the ark carefully on their shoulders, climbed up out of the river bottom to join the others.

Hardly had their feet touched the western bank when a deafening roar sounded from upstream as water crashed down the empty riverbed. Soon the Jordan again overflowed its banks.

For just a moment the people had visions of what would have happened had their God not protected them. How many children would the flooded river have swept away? How many lambs and sheep? How many would have lost their footing and drowned?

But God had protected them, most wonderfully so. The people gazed back across the flooded river. They had left their years of wandering on the other side. The flight from Egypt, the Exodus, was over.

✕ ✕ ✕

The warm, sweet smell of baking batter filled the cozy kitchen. Stacey and Maria sat in front of the stove, watching through the thick glass of the oven door as their cake slowly rose. Jason sat nearby, carefully drawing apples, oranges, and bananas on a piece of paper. When the cake was finished, he wanted to be ready.

"Our next adventure is called 'Commander of the Lord's Army,'" Mr. McDonald announced on the radio. "It's a gripper! So if you're ready, so is Maggie B."

✕ ✕ ✕

Camped at last west of the Jordan, the Israelites worshiped God. With prayer and song and a special meal they celebrated the long-ago night their parents and grandparents had escaped from Egypt. Only a few had lived long enough to actually remember that historic night.

But as campfires flickered, families sat around telling stories of God's leading. They loved to repeat, over and over, God's promise to Abraham. "Lift up your eyes and look north, south, east, and west. All that you see I will give you and your children forever." Now here they were. Back in the land of Abraham.

The next morning people crawled out of their tents, baskets in hand, ready to gather their daily supply of food. But for the first time in 40 years, no sparkling white manna covered the ground.

The people turned blank, puzzled faces to Joshua, who stood there laughing gently, his brown eyes twinkling. "We are in a land of plenty," he reminded them. "You no longer need to look to the sky for food, but to the fruitful earth."

Slow smiles of understanding spread across the people's faces. God would not do for them what they could do for themselves.

Leaving the people to forage for grains and fruits, Joshua wandered off by himself. He needed to talk with God. Much depended on what he did during the next few days. He knew the first step in claiming the land of Canaan was to take the city of Jericho. But how?

Gazing westward, he eyed the city, so close he could see scores of soldiers patrolling its massive walls. From the spies' report, he knew the mud-brick walls were well fortified, thick, and strong. Inside those walls trained, heavily armed forces waited, well prepared for war.

The Israelites would never win against Jericho without a brilliant strategy—if then. But clever as he was, Joshua could think of no plan crafty enough to ensure victory over Jericho.

He realized, of course, that the city was terrified of the Israelites, and that was an advantage. They had felt reasonably safe while the Jordan was at flood stage. So sure were they that the Israelites could not possibly cross it that they hadn't even posted guards along its banks. But they had watched in shock as the Israelites, like an army of ants, had marched across the empty riverbed.

But we didn't do it! Joshua thought. *God did. I may be a good soldier and an able commander, but we're no match for a large, fortified city with well-trained soldiers. How are we to take the city of Jericho?*

Once more he gazed at the city. A never-ending water supply flowed into Jericho from a clear, gushing spring. Acres of date palms surrounded the city. Its large, well-guarded gate was clearly visible, as were the many soldiers marching back and forth along the top of its huge walls. "Dear God," he whispered, "what am I to do?"

He sensed before he saw the presence just behind him. Wheeling, hand on sword, he stared into the face of the most noble warrior he had ever seen. Tall, brawny, but graceful, the soldier fixed him with a gaze that stilled his hand upon the sword. The soldier's gleaming armor glinted in the sunlight and a sword, drawn and held high, beamed with a blinding brightness.

Joshua swallowed hard, but found the courage to demand, "Who are you, friend or foe?"

In a low, powerful voice the soldier answered, "I am the Commander-in-chief of the Lord's army!"

For a split second Joshua stared, not understanding. Then the realization dawned that he was speaking to the Lord Himself.

In an instant he threw himself facedown on the ground, worshiping the Lord and asking, "What will You have me to do? Just give the command, and I will do it!"

"First," the Commander answered, "take off your shoes."

Quickly, reverently, Joshua slipped out of his sandals, thinking fleetingly of Moses' experience at the burning bush. Then the divine Commander bent low and talked to Joshua.

"About Jericho . . ." He began, and Joshua's eyes grew big and round as he listened. The Commander spoke of kings and priests and the sacred ark, and Joshua's eyes sparkled with wonder and excitement.

Never, if he lived to be 1,000, would he have thought of such a wonderful plan for defeating Jericho. Why had he even worried? God, the commander of the army, the ruler of Canaan, the king of the whole universe, was still in charge.

And Jericho was in for a surprise.

✗ ✗ ✗

"I don't have to tell you what happened to that city," Mr. McDonald said into his microphone, his voice traveling by invisible radio waves to the citizens of Valley Springs. "The walls of Jericho came tumblin' down, all because a group of people believed their God. Exciting stuff.

"Now, for our final story this afternoon, Maggie B is going to move us forward in history just a little until we find our hero, Joshua, facing yet another great challenge. Here, once again, is the one and only Maggie B.

Adoni-Zedek, Amorite king of Jerusalem, ran a hand through his rumpled hair. "I don't believe it!" he shouted angrily. "The Gibeonites have made a peace treaty with Israel! The traitors! Why couldn't they have joined with us against the Israelites? This could mean the end of all of us!"

He suddenly whirled and flung an order at a servant. "Send runners with a message to the kings of Hebron, Jarmuth, Lachish, and Eglon. Tell them to deliver this message: 'Come and help the king of Jerusalem destroy Gibeon, for it has made peace with the people of Israel!'"

The runners departed. Soon the four kings listened in astonishment and fear to Adoni-Zedek's message. Swiftly they gathered their armies and prepared to march on Gibeon.

Some time later Joshua was surprised to find some breathless visitors from Gibeon at his tent.

"Come and help us!" they begged. "Quick! All the Amorites of the hill country have gathered to attack us!"

Joshua listened soberly, his dark eyes registering every word. But this time he did not make a decision without talking to the Lord about it. And God told him exactly what to do.

"Go, and don't be afraid of them," the Lord directed, "for they are already defeated, yours to destroy. Not one will be able to stand against you."

Assured that he acted with God's blessing, Joshua quickly rallied his troops and set out toward Gibeon. All night they tramped. A silvery slice of moon rose in the sky and cast eerie shadows through the treetops. The men marched silently, darting glances over their shoulders and trying to see through the gloom ahead. Had the Amorites discovered them? Did they lurk in the shadows, ready to attack?

LOT'S ENEMIES

Below is a list of Lot's enemies. They have been encrypted onto touch-tone telephone buttons. Each button represents one letter in the answer. The correct letter will be one of the three to choose from on the button. (Answers on page 117.)

Hint: All of Lot's enemies are mentioned in this chapter.

ABC	MNO	MNO	PRS	GHI	TUV	DEF	PRS
2	6	6	7	4	8	3	7

JKL	GHI	MNO	GHI	QZ	ABC	DEF	MNO	MNO	GHI	QZ	DEF	DEF	DEF	JKL
5	4	6	4	0	2	3	6	6	4	0	3	3	3	5

JKL	GHI	MNO	GHI	QZ	MNO	DEF	QZ	DEF	GHI	JKL	MNO	MNO
5	4	6	4	0	6	3	0	3	4	5	6	6

JKL	GHI	MNO	GHI	QZ	MNO	DEF	QZ	GHI	DEF	ABC	PRS	MNO	MNO
5	4	6	4	0	6	3	0	4	3	2	7	6	6

JKL	GHI	MNO	GHI	QZ	MNO	DEF	QZ	JKL	ABC	PRS	GHI	GHI	ABC
5	4	6	4	0	6	3	0	5	2	7	4	4	2

JKL	GHI	MNO	GHI	QZ	MNO	DEF	QZ	JKL	ABC	PRS	MNO	TUV	TUV	GHI
5	4	6	4	0	6	3	0	5	2	7	6	8	8	4

But just at daybreak they reached the outskirts of Gibeon without being sighted by the enemy. The unsuspecting Amorites surrounded the city. Without warning, the Israelite army struck them.

Surprised at the sudden attack, the Amorites fought back fiercely, their swords slashing and slicing. But the Israelites battled just as intensely, their arms made strong by a mighty God.

The blazing sun climbed higher in the sky, while the pale moon slipped toward the horizon. The Amorites felt their sword arms grow tired, and great drops of sweat rolled down their faces. But the Israelites, even after marching all night, fought with the strength of fresh troops.

Finally the terrified kings screamed, "Retreat! Retreat!" and the armies turned tail and ran. But which way should they run? Out of habit they turned toward Jerusalem, but Joshua and his army had cut off that way of escape.

Now beside themselves with panic, the kings cried, "Run the other way!" Like so many scurrying mice, they fled—westward toward lower Beth-Horon—with Israel right behind them. Then as they scrambled down toward the lower hill country, a strange thing happened. Great hailstones began to plummet from the sky. They dropped with tremendous force, killing more Amorites than Joshua and all his army had slain.

The Israelite army, close behind, hurried on, the hailstones falling inches from them, but never touching even one soldier. Finally Joshua held up his hand and called a halt. Gazing down at the fleeing Amorites, then at his sweaty soldiers, who had marched all night and fought half the day, he prayed.

"Let the sun stand still over Gibeon, and let the moon stand in its place over the valley of Ajalon!" Joshua's men turned to stare at him in amazement. *What kind of prayer was that?*

But Joshua knew why he prayed, and he knew the Lord understood. He needed more time. Israel needed complete victory. The battle would have to be fought again if he did not finish it today. They needed daylight.

God, of course, could do anything. For hours the Israelites chased the Amorites, for hours they fought them. But the sun seemed not to move at all. The Amorites battled as if in a never-ending nightmare. Exhausted, they stared at the sun. *It hasn't moved!* they thought. *What is going on here? Will this day never end? Will the blistering sun never set?* But the Israelites fought as if refreshed by a breeze from heaven.

Finally, as the five kings saw their armies being slaughtered, they escaped over the hills toward Makkedah. Coming upon a deep, roomy cave, they scooted inside and cowered against the cool stone walls.

The battle was nearly over. Joshua had found how easy it was to win when God fought with him. The sun still shone brightly, and his men still had the strength of a new army.

Suddenly an eager young soldier ran up to him and blurted, "The five kings have escaped and are hiding in a cave in Makkedah!" Joshua nodded, then directed, "Take some men and go roll a large stone over the entrance. We'll deal with them later."

At last the fighting ground to a halt, and the sun, after lighting the sky for a day and a half, finally disappeared in a rosy glow behind the hills. Joshua and the Israelites had defeated five armies, but not one Israelite had died.

As Joshua gazed at the western sky he whispered, "Thank You, Lord. I won't forget this day and your answer to my prayer."

Stacey and Maria lifted the freshly baked cake from the oven as the story ended. It was plump, slightly brown, and absolutely perfect.

Jason eagerly rubbed his hands and quickly licked his lips. "You're about to see cake decorating like you've never seen."

"Hold on, Rembrandt," Stacey giggled. "We'd better let it cool a few minutes. Then you can be creative all you want. I'm going to call the grocery store to make sure they've got the frozen pizzas we need while Maria digs the raw vegetables and dip out of the fridge. We've got less than an hour to get all this stuff ready for the professor's party."

Stacey skipped from the room as Jason eyed the cake. "Now wait for it to cool," he heard her call from the den. "OK?"

"OK," Jason agreed. His artistic impulses were strong. But if cool cakes decorated better than hot cakes, he'd be patient. One thing he was sure of—it would be a creation Professor Appleby would never forget.

② Party Time

Evening shadows were just beginning to spread across the forest as Stacey and her friends arrived at the mansion. Mrs. Roth guided the station wagon to a spot by the front porch and switched off the ignition.

"I don't see Miss Baker's car," she said, glancing about the clearing. "We did invite her, didn't we?"

"Three days ago," her daughter stated, climbing out of the automobile while balancing a pile of gifts in her arms. "She said she was going to get her hair done and everything."

"Oooh," Maria breathed, "that's a good sign. When a woman gets her hair done the very day she's meeting a gentleman friend, it means she thinks he's special."

"Or it could mean she's tired of looking like a witch," Mrs. Roth chuckled. "That's usually my motivation for a visit to the beauty parlor."

Stacey grinned over at her mom. "Seems you weren't so interested in your hair until Mr. McDonald moved to town. Could there be a connection?"

Mrs. Roth blushed slightly. "You just mind your own business," she teased. "Mr. McDonald is a lovely man and I like being with him. As a matter of fact, if he and Marlene weren't visiting a sick aunt this evening, they'd be here helping us celebrate my father's birthday."

"How old is Professor Appleby, anyway?" Maria wanted to know.

Mrs. Roth stopped and thought for a moment. "Why, I believe this is his seventieth birthday. That's right. My father is 70 years old."

"Wow," Maria gasped. "That's a lot of birthdays, huh, Jason?"

"Yeah," the boy said absentmindedly. "A lot."

Stacey walked to the back of the car. "What's with you, Jason? You've been acting kinda strange—ever since you iced the cake. And you won't even let us see it. You've got it all packed away in that plastic cake carrier." She reached out her hand. "How 'bout lettin' us take a peek inside?"

"No!" the boy said, stepping back. "I mean, not yet. It's . . . it's . . . not ready."

"Not ready? You're not finished?"

"That's right. Got a few more fruits to put on it. Then we can give it to the professor."

"How about the candles?" Maria asked. "We've got to put some candles on the cake."

"I'll do that, too. Just don't worry about it, OK?"

Stacey shrugged. "Well, OK. I guess you can be in charge of the candles as well. Besides, Maria and I have our hands full with all these gifts and other party preparations. Just make it really beautiful. You turn 70 only once, you know."

Jason nodded slowly. "Yeah. It'll be . . . very nice. I promise."

The small band of partygoers hurried across the lawn and climbed the broad steps leading to the front porch. "Hey, Grandfather," Stacey called through the screen door. "We're here."

"Who's here?" came the distant reply.

"We are. Stacey? Maria? Jason? Your daughter—you know, my mom?"

"Sorry. Can't come to the door. I'm watching television."

The group stood in confused silence for a moment. "Wait a minute," Maria whispered. "The professor doesn't even *have* a television. He thinks they're time-stealers. I've heard him say so."

"You're right," Stacey breathed. Turning back to the doorway, she called, "You don't have a television set, Grandfather. So how can you be watching it?"

A long pause. "Good point," came the reply.

"So," the girl continued, "why don't you come down and see who's at your front door?"

Another long pause. "Well, OK. But you can't stay long. I'm expecting my granddaughter and her mother to stop by any minute now. It's my birthday. I'm 60 years old."

Mrs. Roth smiled. "Aren't you underestimating things just a tad?"

Footsteps sounded down a long, unseen hallway. "I ought to know how old I am. After all, I've been me a lot longer than anyone else has."

Maria giggled. "Can't argue with that."

A moment later a smiling face appeared at the doorway. "Well, if it isn't my granddaughter Stacey and her beautiful mother. Come on in. Hello, Maria. Hi, Jason. You folks didn't happen to see anyone else out there? Had visitors a few minutes ago. Kept insisting I don't have a television."

Mrs. Roth opened her mouth to speak, then sighed. Reaching out, she gave her father a hug. She refused to play along with his joke. He might be absentminded, but he didn't have to exaggerate it so. "You look nice tonight, Dad. Expecting anyone special?"

Professor Appleby shrugged. "Maybe I am, maybe I'm not."

Maria grinned. "You am," she said.

They entered the big mansion and made their way to the cozy kitchen, where preparations immediately began for the long-awaited event. Soon brightly colored balloons fluttered from paper streamers and the warm tomato smell of fresh pizza baking filled the house.

Jason, unlike his usual outgoing nature, secluded himself in the small pantry. "I've got more creating to do," he told the others. "The cake isn't the way I want it yet."

Stacey frowned as the boy closed the door behind him. It wasn't like her friend to be by himself, especially when party preparations were involved. She shook her head and chuckled softly to herself, "Artists. They're a weird bunch."

A car horn tooted outside just as Maria and Mrs. Roth were putting the finishing touches on the tossed salad.

"I'll get it!" Professor Appleby announced with a little more enthusiasm than usual. "I mean, I'll go see who's just arrived. It may be someone needing directions into town. Folks tend to get lost in these parts, you know."

Stacey grinned. "You do that, Grandfather. And tell Miss Baker we could use some help in the kitchen."

The old man blinked innocently. "Oh, yes. Miss Baker. That may be her. I'd almost forgotten she was coming."

Mrs. Roth patted her father on the back. "Dad," she said maternally, "don't fib in front of the children. You might warp their characters."

Professor Appleby lifted his hands. "I'm an old man," he said.

"My mind isn't as sharp as it used to be."

Mrs. Roth smiled. "It's not your mind we're dealing with here, Dad," she said, reaching up and brushing stray strands of snow-white hair from his forehead. "It's your heart. Love is timeless. It doesn't celebrate birthdays." She paused and looked deeply into her father's eyes. "Love is forever young."

Professor Appleby returned his daughter's gaze. "What would your mother say about this?"

Mrs. Roth slipped her arms around the professor. "If she were alive, she wouldn't have to say anything. Miss Baker would be just another friend of the family. But Mom has been gone for a long, long time. And I know she would never, ever want you to be lonely if there was someone who was willing to love your mind and your heart as she did."

Outside another *toot-toot* echoed across the clearing. A soft, gentle smile covered the old man's face. "Is it OK for me to feel this way?" he asked.

"It's OK, Father," the woman replied. "No, it's more than OK. It's time."

Professor Appleby held his daughter close to him for a long moment. Then he turned and hurried out of the kitchen. Stacey saw her mother brush a tear from her cheek and head for the oven. The pizzas should be just about done.

"Hello, Professor," the cheery voice of Miss Anna Baker called when she saw her friend emerge from the house. "Sorry to sit here tooting my horn like a teenager, but I've got more in here than I can carry. Guess I need some help."

The woman squeezed her plump body from behind the wheel and opened the back door of her little car. "Lot of folks at the community college asked me to relay their greetings—and gifts. Seems you've got quite a fan club among the faculty."

Professor Appleby gasped when he saw the back seat covered with brightly wrapped boxes of many sizes and shapes. "Well, well," he said. "Will you look at all that loot. Now, you be sure to tell these kind people how much I appreciate their thoughtfulness."

"And I got you something too," Miss Baker said shyly, adjusting the hairpin keeping her gray-streaked hair in place above her head. "Nothing to get all excited about. Just a reminder of my respect and regard for one of Valley Springs' favorite citizens." She paused. "Mind if I give it to you out here instead of inside? It's so little, it might get lost in the shuffle."

"Sure," the old man replied. "Which one is it?"

"I didn't have time to wrap it," Miss Baker stated. "Got it from the engraver just now. That's why I'm a little late. Poor man had to stay open after hours. But when he found out whom it was for, he didn't mind."

"Engraver? What'd ya do, buy me a tombstone?"

The woman laughed. "Oh, nothing as depressing as that." She reached into her purse. "I know you do a lot of writing to your sister Maggie B, so I thought you might like this." She withdrew her hand. Held tightly in her fingers was a shiny gold fountain pen, its polished surface reflecting the porch light like a mirror. "Your daughter said you're not one for computers and such. She said you like to write the old-fashioned way—with ink pen and all." Miss Baker paused. "Do you like it?"

Professor Appleby gingerly took the writing instrument from his friend's outstretched hand. "Will you look at this. I've never seen such a fine fountain pen in all my 60 years."

Miss Baker blinked. "Aren't you more like 70 years old?"

"Details, details," the professor said, turning the golden device in his hand, watching it catch the light and flash it back at him. "You're only as old as you feel. And I feel more like 60 than 70 today. Especially in such lovely company."

His companion blushed and pointed shyly. "Do you see the engraving? It's right there on the cover."

The old man lifted the pen closer to his face and turned so the porch light shone directly over his shoulder. "Yes. I see it."

"Well," Miss Baker urged, "go ahead and read it. I won't mind."

Professor Appleby adjusted his glasses and grinned. "It's not mushy or anything, is it?"

"Maybe. Maybe not," came the quick reply.

"Let's see," the man said. "It says, 'To my friend Professor Appleby. May the words you write bring as much joy as the words you speak. Anna.'"

"I'm a history teacher," the woman said softly. "Not a poet."

"It's . . ." Professor Appleby cleared his throat. "It's the most beautiful thing anyone has said to me for a long, long time. Thank you."

A gentle wind whispered through the leaves overhead as a nighthawk whistled its call somewhere in the starry sky. Wordlessly the two friends gathered the gifts from the back of Miss Baker's car and climbed the steps leading into the yellow glow of the mansion. They had a party to attend. But for Professor Appleby the celebration would include more than the passing of years. This evening, surrounded by family and friends, he'd be caroling a song of his own—a timeless melody every heart longs to sing.

✗ ✗ ✗

As the last pieces of pizza disappeared down eager throats and the salad bowl held only remnants of lettuce leaves and tomato slices, Stacey and Maria looked over at Jason expectantly. It was time for him to bring the cake in from its hiding place in the pantry.

Mrs. Roth slid her chair back from the table and sighed. "I would like to thank the Italians personally for inventing pizza."

"I heard someplace that pizza was invented in San Francisco, California," Miss Baker stated.

"Hey," Mrs. Roth announced, lifting her hands, "it could have been developed by a Russian sailor on the Black Sea, for all I care. I'd love it anyway."

"Yeah," Maria agreed. "Pizza is almost as good as my mother's vegetable burritos smothered in hot tomato sauce with pieces of jalapeño pepper sliced in it and—"

"Hold it!" Stacey interrupted. "If I even think about more food, I'll pop. I've saved just enough room for a piece of birthday cake and that's it. So, Jason, how 'bout it?"

"How 'bout what?" the boy asked.

"How 'bout you go into your secret laboratory—better known as Professor Appleby's pantry—and bring out your great creation? You've kept us in suspense long enough."

Jason lifted his chin. "It's not done yet."

"*What?*" Stacey rose two inches above her chair. "How can it not be done yet? You've been working on that cake all afternoon!"

"Art takes time."

"So does mold," the girl shot back.

Jason stuck to his guns. "It's not ready and won't be until I say so."

Stacey sighed in frustration. "Jason," she said quietly through clenched teeth. "It took God only seven days to create the entire world. While I understand you're not the Creator, some things just shouldn't take so long. Decorating a cake is one of 'em."

Jason closed his eyes. Stacey's heart skipped a beat when she realized her friend was on the verge of crying. "I want it to be perfect," he said with difficulty. "Right now it isn't. Please. Let me finish it."

"Sure, Jason," Stacey replied, casting a worried look at her mother. "Whatever you say."

Professor Appleby frowned slightly, unsure of what was going on. "I know," he brightened suddenly. "How 'bout if I give *you* guys a surprise while Jason is putting the finishing touches on my cake? Maggie B sent some new tapes. I haven't even had time to take them to Mr. McDonald at the station yet. Want to hear them?"

"Yes!" Stacey and Maria shouted.

"Sounds good to me," Mrs. Roth stated. "It'll give my supper a little time to settle."

"What are they about?" Miss Baker wanted to know.

"Beats me," Professor Appleby said, rising to his feet. "Haven't even heard them myself. I'll get the machine, and we can enjoy them right here in the kitchen. Jason can do his thing in the pantry while they're playing."

Within minutes the table had been cleared and Professor Appleby's cassette tape recorder sat center stage surrounded by eager faces and willing ears. Jason slipped into the confines of the pantry and left the door open slightly so he could hear.

"This first one is called 'A Woman Goes to War,'" the old man announced. "Sounds exciting. Everybody ready?"

"Ready!" came the enthusiastic reply from those at the table. "Ready," came the disembodied response from the direction of the pantry.

"OK," Professor Appleby stated, placing the cassette into the machine. "Maggie B, we're all yours."

✗ ✗ ✗

Joshua was gone. And his worst fears had come true. Many who had promised to serve God faithfully had broken their promise and had begun to worship idols.

But God still did not forget them. Even while they worshiped the gods of Canaan, He sent special people, prophets and judges, to help them out of their troubles and give them advice. Usually He chose men, because practically everyone at that time thought men were more important, and so people paid more attention to what a man had to say.

But after years of peace here, war there, of endless fighting between God's people and the Canaanites, God called a woman. And although everyone was shocked that He picked a woman to work for Him, no one was surprised that the woman was Deborah.

Deborah stood out from the crowd. Not that she looked unusual. Her black hair framed an oval face with a no-nonsense mouth, strong nose, and intelligent brown eyes. Those eyes often held a twinkle, and the jut of her jaw suggested a strong person-

ality. But her looks were not remarkably different from those of other Israelite women.

Nor did Deborah command attention because she had married an important man, had a lot of children, or created scrumptious stews in her cooking pot. She stood out because of her fiery spirit, totally dedicated to God and His people.

The first time she received a message from Him she could hardly believe that God had spoken to her! The wonder of it was so great that she fell to the hard-packed earth and worshiped Him. But when she arose, she delivered God's message with a strong voice and fearless eye.

People found her courageous and firm, one who would always speak the truth, no matter what. Yet Deborah knew how to sympathize with them in their troubles. They began to come to her for good advice and thought of her as a wise and kindly mother, filled with God's Spirit. And each day more and more people crowded around her, eager to have her settle some matter that no one else could handle.

In time she picked a special spot under a palm tree as her own outdoor courtroom. By now all Israel looked to her as their prophet and their judge. With God's help Deborah settled arguments among families, neighbors, and even between the different tribes. But she didn't know what to do about the constant attacks upon them by the people of Canaan.

It surprised the Canaanites to see how Israel had settled into the land. Many times before they had seen nomads come and go. One day they would be there, grazing their sheep and setting up their tents. The next they would be gone, with little more than a tramped-down field and a circle of stones to show that they had ever been there at all.

But the Israelites were different. Instead of putting up tents, they erected huts of mud-brick or stone. They cut down trees, clearing land in the dense but scrubby forests of the hill country. Planting crops, they remained to harvest them. "These people plan to stay!" the Canaanites told each other in alarm. And of course they did, for God had given them the land.

But the people of Canaan were determined to make them pay for the right to live in the hill country. Time after time they attacked the Israelites, punishing them with arrows and swords, hoping they would offer lots of booty to make the Canaanites leave them alone. God's people lived in constant fear. They dared not travel the main roads, but slipped along crooked little pathways, afraid of attack. Many hid in the mountains. But here too the Canaanites persecuted them, even pressing some of them into slavery.

In the northern part of Canaan sprawled the great walled city of Hazor. Its king, Jabin, had oppressed the Israelites for 20 years. Now he decided to launch such a strong attack against the northern and central tribes that they would pay tribute forever. He assembled a huge army with 900 war chariots and put them under the command of his most capable general, Sisera.

In this crisis Deborah prayed. And God told her what to do. She arose from her knees with the light of battle in her eyes. Immediately she sent for Barak, a member of the tribe of Naphtali.

"This is what God wants you to do," she told him. "Gather 10,000 men from the tribes of Naphtali and Zebulun. Lead them to Mount Tabor. God will lead the Canaanites to the valley by the Kishon River. When his troops and chariots dash into the valley, the Lord will deliver them into your hands."

Barak gasped. *Attack Sisera?* What was the woman thinking of? He knew the Lord gave her special messages, but could this one be right? He thought about those 900 war chariots. And the thought left him weak with fear. Those chariots, pulled by swift horses, would each carry two warriors, experts with the bow and arrow.

The Canaanite soldiers would be covered with armor, including helmets. But the Israelite soldiers had no armor, except for some leather-covered shields. And while the Canaanite soldiers carried spears and long-range bows, the Israelites still fought with simple weapons.

Barak wanted to say, "No, I won't do it. The Canaanites are far better equipped for war. We'll all be slaughtered!" But Deborah's blazing eyes dared him to back out. And he couldn't.

Instead, he stammered, "I'll go if you'll go with me. But if you don't go, I won't go."

Deborah gave him a withering stare that said, *Barak, where is your faith in God?* But she answered, "Of course I'll go with you. And Israel will win the battle. But the road you travel will not lead to glory. You will not receive honor for the victory. The credit will go to a woman."

Barak frowned over those strange words. Whoever heard of a woman receiving credit for winning a battle? But he had no time to worry about that. He had to round up 10,000 men. And the task would not be easy.

The day of battle arrived. Israelite troops, 10,000 men from the tribes of Naphtali and Zebulun, joined by a few from the tribes of Issachar, Ephraim, Manasseh, and Benjamin, spread out over the hills rimming the Kishon Valley. Only in the hills would they have any protection from Canaanite war chariots. At Barak's command, they gathered together at Mount Tabor.

Deborah, in the meantime, led a small group of troops into the valley below. It was the most dangerous place to be. The flat land provided the perfect surface for galloping horses and chariot wheels.

She prayed at every step. God would give them this battle. She had no doubt of it. But she must be alert, watchful, for His messages to her.

Then Sisera struck, his vast army filling the valley. Her eyes narrowed as she saw clouds of dust and then heard thundering hoofbeats. The Canaanites were coming. Sisera's army thought that all the Israelite troops were in the valley, and they had come to destroy them.

Deborah kept praying. Then she saw a most unusual sight. Storm clouds! At the height of the dry season, black rain-filled clouds swirled over the hills and swooped toward the valley. With a joyous shout Deborah gave Barak her signal. And at that signal Israelite soldiers swarmed down the slope.

Thunder rolled. Then the rain struck, falling fast and hard. The solid clay soil under Deborah's feet turned soft. In a panic the chariot drivers began to whip their horses as hundreds of wheels began to sink in the mud.

And all the while the Israelite foot soldiers hurtled down the slope of Mount Tabor toward them. The chariots lumbered onward, mud clinging to their wheels. No longer swift-moving vehicles of death, they struggled across the plain like giant beetles in a sea of honey. With the Israelites close behind them, they headed west toward the Wadi Kishon.

WHAT BARAK LEARNED

Each symbol in the answers represents a letter of the alphabet. Write the answers to each clue with one letter under each symbol. Using your answers, decode the secret message at the bottom of the page to discover what Barak learned. (Answers are on page 117.)

Prophetess

Enemy leader

Tribe that helped send 10,000 men

Tools of war

God's way to slow the chariots

Gushing streams raced down the hills and poured into the wadi, which should have been nearly dry at that time of year. Suddenly it became a raging river of foaming brown water.

By now the valley floor had turned into mud soup, thick and sticky. Horses reared and whinnied as their chariots overturned or sank so deep into the muck that they could not move. Panic-stricken soldiers jumped from the chariots and slogged through the mud, trying to get away from that oncoming army of Israelites avalancing down toward them.

The marshy ground around the wadi stood in water. The rain drove down in great, gray sheets. Then—a sudden roar as the wadi overflowed its banks. Chariot drivers, chariots and horses, and Canaanite soldiers with all their armor disappeared beneath the flood. A few stragglers escaped the waters, but Israelite soldiers quickly found and destroyed them.

But they did not capture General Sisera. Realizing what was about to happen, he had headed northward, escaping the flood and the Israelites.

Shocked, unable to believe that his marvelous army had met with such disaster, he headed for a place he thought he had friends who would protect him from Barak. At last he reached a tent in which he thought he'd be safe. Exhausted, he lay down and went to sleep. But while he was sleeping, a woman known by the name of Jael crept close to his mat and killed him.

Deborah sang a song of victory. God had once again worked a miracle. And Deborah's prophecy had come true. Sisera, the skillful general, had met his death at the hands of a woman. And the human glory for destroying an enemy of God's people would go not to fearful Barak, but to Jael, the woman of Deborah's prophecy.

✕ ✕ ✕

"Wow, that was kinda scary," Maria gasped. "I sure wouldn't want to go through such a terrible ordeal."

"Me neither," Stacey agreed.

"Me too," Jason called from behind the pantry door.

Professor Appleby lifted the next cassette and read what was written on its label. "Looks like this one's the story of my favorite

Old Testament Bible character, Gideon. It's called 'Wet Fleece, Dry Fleece.' It's a two-parter, so we'd better get listening."

✕ ✕ ✕

Throughout Canaan the tribes of Israel sat back with satisfied smiles. They ignored God's command to drive idol worship, with its evil practices, out of the land, and they felt too lazy and contented to fight any more wars.

Instead of moving their flocks and herds from pasture to pasture as they had for so many years, they happily settled in one place and became farmers. They planted crops and harvested the groves and vineyards that had fallen into their hands when Joshua had led them against the Canaanites.

But Joshua was gone. No one had taken his place. The tribes squabbled among themselves and soon forgot their promise to serve the Lord. Before long some made friends with the idol worshipers and even married some of them.

The Israelites watched, horrified, as the Canaanites sacrificed their own children, or danced around the temple to Asherah. But slowly, gradually, many of the Israelites began to worship those gods too. And just as Joshua had warned, trouble came. Powerful neighboring tribes raided the Israelite villages, killing, stealing, destroying.

But God had not forgotten His children, although He grieved when they turned their backs on Him. He sent special people called judges to guide them and give them messages.

Then for a time the people would be sorry for their wicked ways and repent. But when the green barley waved in the breeze, and the lambs frolicked on the hillsides, and every cooking pot was full, the people again forgot their loving God.

Now His people suffered again, this time at the hands of the Midianites, the Amalekites, and other tribes gathered in the eastern desert. Like swarms of locusts they swept westward, attacking everything in their way.

Thousands of nomads suddenly appeared as if from nowhere. Led by richly robed chiefs on swift, sure-footed camels, they looted food supplies, sheep, oxen, and donkeys. With fierce, wild cries they seized or drove away peacefully grazing flocks and used the pasture for their own animals. Then as swiftly as they came, they disappeared, leaving nothing behind but ruin.

The tribe of Manasseh lay directly in their path. Now God's people cowered in caves, hiding from the Midianites. They hid their scant supplies of grain in nooks and crannies in the rocks. Children cried from hunger, and grown-ups forgot how to smile. Heads bowed low, they begged God to save them.

And God heard their prayers. One day Gideon, of the tribe of Manasseh, bent over a pitiful little bunch of wheat. Hiding by a winepress away from the eyes of the Midianites, he threshed the wheat, beating the tough, yellow stems with a stick.

As the few golden kernels fell to the ground, he thought miserably of the acres of wheat he and his family had planted and cared for. But the Midianites had waited just until harvesttime, then pounced. Now of all his family's beautiful wheat, only a few scattered stalks remained. *God has forsaken us,* he thought.

But even as he threshed the grain and brooded, Someone was watching him. Suddenly Gideon heard a voice saying, "Mighty soldier, the Lord is with you!" He looked up to see a stranger sitting under an oak tree.

Gideon jumped with fright. Had the Midianites discovered his hiding place? No, the man didn't look like a Midianite. But what did his strange words mean? *I'm no mighty soldier!* he thought. And he almost laughed at the words "The Lord is with you!"

A faint smile twisted the corners of his mouth as he answered, "Stranger, if the Lord is with us, why have all these bad things happened? And where are all the miracles our ancestors told us about?"

The visitor smiled into Gideon's questioning eyes. "You, Gideon," he replied, "will save Israel. Go, and I will make you strong!"

Gideon blinked. *That's impossible!* he thought. *And just who is this stranger, anyway?*

"I come from a poor, unimportant family," Gideon exclaimed, "and I'm the least important one in it! How can I possibly save Israel?"

But the stranger promised, "I, the Lord, will be with you, and you shall defeat the Midianites."

Gideon's heart thumped wildly. He was talking to the Lord! Or was he? How could he be sure?

But deep inside he knew that his visitor was somehow special. Remembering his manners, the code of hospitality, he ran to prepare some food. Even though he had barely enough for his own family, he prepared the best he had.

At last he returned to the stranger with a basket of roast goat, a pot of broth, and a stack of bread. The stranger, in the guise of an ordinary man, looked right into Gideon's mind. *He doesn't quite believe who I am,* God thought. Aloud He said, "Place the meat and the bread upon that rock over there, and pour the broth over it." Puzzled, Gideon obeyed.

Without a word the stranger lifted his staff and touched the bread and the meat. Instantly flames leaped out of the gray rock and burned up the wet food.

After that Gideon felt he couldn't do enough for the Lord. Following the stranger's directions, he took 10 strong men and climbed to the top of a hill where an altar to Baal sprawled under a starry sky. Straining, pushing, pounding, hacking, the men broke apart the mud-cemented stones. Then Gideon harnessed a 7-year-old bull, an animal often used as a sacrifice to Baal, to the great stones and scattered them all over the hillside.

When the Baal worshipers discovered what Gideon had done, they were angry enough to kill him. A crowd gathered around the cave where Joash, Gideon's father, hid from the Midianites. "Bring out your son!" they bellowed. "He must die for his insult to Baal!"

Joash's bulky form loomed in the opening. "Oh, does Baal need someone to defend him? You mean he can't take care of himself? Perhaps you're the ones who should die for insulting him! He might not appreciate your notion that he can't defend himself!" Gideon's father taunted them.

Confused, and muttering under their breath, people in the crowd slunk away.

But Gideon had no time or thought for false gods or angry crowds. The Lord had told him to form an army and attack the Midianites. *I can't do it!* he thought. *How can I attack thousands of warriors racing about on camels? And how can I be sure that the Lord is with me?*

"I know!" he finally exclaimed under his breath. "I'll ask the Lord for a sign."

That night as Gideon lifted his gaze to the starry sky, he prayed. "Lord, if You really want me to save Israel, prove it to me in this way. I'll put some wool on the threshing floor, and if it's wet in the morning, while all the ground around it is dry, I'll know You are going to help me!"

Carefully he spread a thick, wooly fleece, dry as ashes, on the threshing floor. Then, almost too excited to fall asleep, he crawled into a cave and wrapped himself in his own wool cloak for the night.

With the first pale hint of morning, Gideon jumped up and raced to the threshing floor—then stood stock still. He hardly dared to look.

What if God had not heard his prayer? What if everything was damp with dew, just as usual? But gathering his courage, he edged closer. Finally he bent over and touched the fleece. Wet—soaking, dripping, wet. Face flushed with excitement, he ran his hand across the ground under and around the fleece. Dry—dry as sawdust. Wonderingly he picked up the fleece and squeezed a whole bowlful of water out of it.

"He did it!" he shouted to the morning. "God answered my prayer and did just what I asked!" Then he sat down on the dry threshing floor with a big, happy grin on his face. But as his excitement began to wear off, he started to think.

I didn't ask God for a very good test. I should have asked for a dry fleece with a wet floor. After all, everyone knows that wool absorbs moisture and the dew is heavy at night! He tried to forget those thoughts, but they kept bothering him. *God did just what I asked,* he kept telling himself, but somehow he wasn't satisfied.

Fearfully, somewhat astonished at his own nerve, he again prayed. "Lord, please don't be angry with me, but do You think You could prove Yourself to me in one more test? This time I'd like to have the fleece dry, and everything around it wet. If You do that, I'll know You are with me."

Again Gideon spread a dry fleece, and again he tossed and turned, waiting for morning. The stars had not yet faded from the sky when he hurried toward the threshing floor.

This time he was so eager to touch the fleece that he stumbled and sprawled across it. The soft wool enfolded his body like a cloud—like a soft *dry* cloud. Still lying on the fleece, Gideon let his hand fall to the ground. A smile of pure delight flashed across his face and lit his dancing eyes as he raised and shook his dripping fingers. He had never before seen the threshing floor so wet.

"Now I know that You are with me, God," he prayed as he bowed before the Lord on the little island of dry fleece. "I will do whatever You ask."

⚔ ⚔ ⚔

"I don't think we've heard the last of Gideon," Miss Baker stated. "What's on the next tape, Professor?"

The old man chuckled. "You sound like one of the children, Miss Baker."

"Well, with Maggie B stories in the tape recorder, everyone can be young again."

"How's it going, Jason?" the professor called.

"I'll be ready after this next tape."

"Finally," Stacey breathed, casting a quick glance at Maria. "Give a guy a cake and some icing and he becomes Leonardo da Vinci."

"Hush up," her mother whispered with a frown. "We don't want to hurt Jason's feelings."

"I just want to eat some cake," Stacey countered. "But I'll keep my comments to myself. Sorry."

Miss Baker leaned forward. "Do you think we should go in there and help him?" she asked.

Maria shook her head. "Not Jason. He's kinda stubborn. Wants to do everything by himself. We'd better just listen to the next story and see what happens."

Professor Appleby slipped a tape into the machine and held up his hand. "OK, everyone. Here we go. It's called 'Too Many Men.'" His index finger fell with a click onto the play button. Almost immediately Maggie B's voice joined the party again.

⚔ ⚔ ⚔

Gideon's army of 32,000 men stood facing their leader. They

still felt a little surprised at themselves for even being in an army. And even more surprised to find themselves accepting Gideon as their commander.

It wasn't that he didn't look the part. Tall, handsome, with wavy brown hair and flashing eyes, he might easily have passed for a prince.

But he was just a nobody, Joash's youngest son, a quiet fellow who worked hard and minded his own business. But here they were, staring into Gideon's blazing eyes and taking orders from him. Many thought, *What am I doing here? If I had the nerve, I'd walk away. Gideon's crazy for thinking we can defeat the Midianites, and I must be even crazier for listening to him.*

Gideon was busy with his own thoughts as he gazed back at his hastily gathered army. *I know the Lord is with me, but we have only 32,000 men to throw against a Midianite force of 135,000!*

But he remembered the fire from the rock, the wet fleece, and the dry fleece. God's words, "Go and save Israel, and I will make you strong!" still rang in his ears.

Dismissing his men to make camp, Gideon wandered over to the still-flowing stream of Harod. Stretching himself along the steep, tree-covered bank, he felt the peace of the place surround him. The soft murmur of the brook, the *cheep-cheep-cheep* of fluttering wagtails, soothed his restless thoughts.

Rousing himself at last, he turned his gaze to the limestone hills. The rolling ridge of Mount Carmel merged with the western sky. The Gilboa mountain ridge, at his back, stood as solid as the arm of God.

Finally he lowered his gaze to the opposite side of the Jezreel valley, to the foot of Mount Moreh, where Midianite tents littered the landscape. *They've left themselves only one escape route,* Gideon noted with satisfaction. *And if we should have to escape, their camels won't be able to follow us into these steep and rocky hills.*

Then Gideon heard God's voice. "Your army has far too many men. If all of you go to fight the Midianites, Israel will boast that they saved themselves by their own strength. So go to your men and send home any that are timid and frightened."

Gideon gulped. *Too many men? How could an army have too*

many men? And doesn't God know that the Midianites outnumber us more than four to one?

But he remembered the wet fleece and the dry fleece, and he decided to trust God. "I'm sure God knows what He's doing!" he told himself.

"Men," he shouted to his troops, "if any of you are frightened of the Midianites, if you don't think we can win this battle, go home now!"

The soldiers looked at each other. Then without a word they turned and scurried back toward home. Gideon's mouth dropped open. He had expected some to leave, but most of his army was disappearing right before his eyes. Quickly calculating the number who had left, he was astonished to find that 22,000 men had deserted him. "Twenty-two thousand!" he groaned.

But to his surprise, God spoke again. "Gideon, you still have far too many men. Now take them down to the brook and let them have a quick drink before going to battle. But watch them. If a man takes the time to kneel down to drink, he is not the kind of soldier you need. But if he breaks his stride only long enough to scoop some water in his hand, then drinks from it as he goes, keep him."

Amazed at these directions, Gideon obeyed. And he watched closely. Thousands of his already small army not only knelt on the bank, but stretched themselves full-length on their stomachs.

Gideon's voice rang out. "All you who stopped to drink—go home!"

The men turned blank faces toward Gideon and the few soldiers who surrounded him, those who had merely lapped water from their hands as they hurried toward the enemy. But the rest didn't wait around to ask questions. They turned and ran toward home.

"Now," said Gideon as he faced what remained of his army, "let us see what the Lord will do."

The men looked at each other with shining eyes. Of all Gideon's army, only they remained. Ten, 20, 30 . . . Quickly they counted. Three hundred. God had chosen just 300 men to defeat thousands of Midianites.

That night Gideon took his servant, Purah, and crept to the

edge of the Midianite camp. As they crouched in the darkness, listening to the conversation inside a tent, they heard the troubled voice of a Midianite soldier.

"I just had a weird dream!" they heard him telling someone. "I dreamed that a monstrous loaf of barley bread came tumbling into our camp and struck a tent with such force that it knocked it flat. Now, what do you suppose that means?"

"I know what it means," another voice answered in gloomy tones. "It represents the sword of Gideon! An Israelite, the son of Joash, will attack us in the name of his god, and destroy us!"

Gideon waited to hear no more. Any doubt that God was with him disappeared. The acres and acres of Midianite tents threw no fear into his soul. The countless numbers of camels impressed him no more than if they had been slow-moving sheep. "God is with me! God is with me!" he sang as his feet flew over the rough hills toward his own small camp.

Bursting into camp, he yelled, "Get up! The Lord has given the Midianites into our hands!"

His shadowy form, his voice, his eyes, fairly crackled with excitement. "Follow my lead and do exactly what I do!" he instructed.

In the stillness of midnight three bands of Israelite soldiers, numbering 100 each, positioned themselves around the Midianite camp. Each soldier carried a clay jar and a ram's horn. Hidden inside each jar, an oil-soaked torch hissed and burned.

Straining his eyes in the darkness, Gideon at last saw what he had been waiting for. Midianite guards turned and stumbled sleepily toward their tents, while other soldiers shuffled to take their places.

Eyes blazing and heart pounding, Gideon signaled his own band of men. One hundred trumpets suddenly blasted the still air. Two hundred more echoed noisily from this spot and that, until the night air rang and the camp vibrated with the sound.

The Midianites, confused, alarmed, rolled out of their tents only to be frightened by a sudden flash of light as the army of Gideon broke their jars and waved their torches high. Then a mighty shout escaped 300 Israelite throats as they exclaimed, "For the Lord and for Gideon!"

The sound of smashed jars, the blare of trumpets, and the

gleam of blazing torches in the darkness sent the Midianites rac-
ing in panic-stricken circles. "We're surrounded!" they screamed.
Thousands of sleepy camels filled the air with their snarls as they
flung themselves to their feet and stampeded in all directions.
Fleeing Midianites mistook each other for the enemy and cut
down their own people. Gideon and his men, unhurt, safe in
God's care, chased the Midianites out of their land. Once again
Israel had peace.

✗ ✗ ✗

"OK, everyone," Jason called from the pantry. "Turn off the
lights. I'm about to bring the cake out."

"Hurray!" Stacey and Maria shouted. "Da Vinci's finished."

"Just turn out the lights so you can see the candles."

Mrs. Roth hurried to the doorway and flipped the switch,
plunging the room into darkness except for an eerie glow coming
from the pantry. "I've got most of them lit," the boy said. "Just
hold on a few more seconds." The glow brightened slightly.
"There. All done. Here I come!"

Everyone started to sing the birthday song as Jason emerged
from the pantry with what seemed like a miniature bonfire held
in his outstretched hands. The cake was ablaze with light.

"Happy birthday to you," the group sang with gusto, "happy
birthday to you." Jason moved slowly toward the table. "Happy
birthday, Professor Ap-ple-by." The boy gently placed the burning
object before them. "Happy birthday to you."

A cheer arose from the assembled guests. "Blow out the candles," Miss Baker urged. "See if you can get them all."

The old man closed his eyes momentarily, then reared back,
his lungs filling with air. With his mighty puff all the flames bent
sideways, then flickered out, leaving the room in utter darkness.

"You did it!" Stacey shouted with glee. "You did it, Grandfather. Every one of those candles is out. You may be old, but you
still breathe good."

Mrs. Roth stumbled back through the darkness to the doorway. "Now you'll get your wish," she called, her hand searching
for the switch.

As the kitchen lights came on, everyone gasped. The cake,

besides having the appearance of a porcupine under its load of candles, looked as if someone had hit it with a sledgehammer. Parts of the two-layered structure had collapsed. Icing lay in scattered blobs about the crumbling surface. Someone had desperately tried to prop up portions of the mess with toothpicks. Instead of a perfectly formed cake with colorful pictures of fruit, as the children had envisioned, what lay before them was a complete and utter decorating disaster.

"Jason!" Stacey breathed. "What happened to our cake?"

No answer. He had vanished.

Professor Appleby lifted his hand. "I'll take care of this. You all just sit tight, OK?"

Stacey and Maria nodded. Miss Baker looked over at her friends, an encouraging smile lighting her face.

The old man made his way to the front porch. Out in the darkness he could hear someone softly sobbing, the sound clearly coming from a broken heart.

"Jason?" he called.

No response.

"Jason? May I talk to you for a minute?" He paused. "It's my birthday, you know. I'm entitled to one wish."

"So?"

"So I wish to talk to you."

After a long moment a voice said in the darkness, "I'm sorry I ruined your cake."

"You mean you didn't *want* it to look like that?"

"Of course not. It's terrible."

Professor Appleby sat down on the step and spoke into the darkness. "What happened?"

"I . . . I tried to ice it before it was cool enough. It started coming apart, and I couldn't stop it. The more icing I smeared on, the worse it got. I even tried putting some toothpicks inside, thinking maybe they'd help it stand up, but nothing I did seemed to make any difference. I ruined your birthday, Professor Appleby, and I'm really sorry."

The old man gazed into the night shadows. "Please come sit beside me, Jason. I want to see your face when I talk to you."

A long pause. "I'm ashamed," the boy said.

"Ashamed of what?"

"Of ruining your party. Stacey and Maria will laugh at me and never let me do anything with them again. They probably hate me for what I did to the cake. It was an accident. Really. I didn't do it on purpose. I wanted you to have a beautiful cake with pictures of fruit on it and everything."

Professor Appleby nodded. "I'm sure it would have been the coolest cake I'd ever seen."

A dark form appeared just outside the glow cast by the porch light. "I was going to put icing apples on the top, with some bananas at the edge and strawberries all around the bottom," Jason continued. "Then I was going to write 'Happy Birthday, Professor Appleby' in red letters along the side."

"Oh, that would've been excellent—a real work of art."

"Yeah. Well, now it just looks like I sat on it."

The old man chuckled. "Sort of reminds me of what we all do to Jesus," he said.

"What do you mean?" the boy asked. "I never tried to decorate a cake for Him."

"Oh, but we try to decorate something else. We say, 'Hey, God, I'm going to live a perfect life for You. I'm going to be kind and forgiving and not get mad or say bad things or think evil thoughts.' Then we get busy with our dream, and suddenly life begins to crumble right in our hands. We try our best, our very best. But we make mistakes, sometimes dreadful ones, and end up with a pretty sad mess—just like your cake.

"Then we try to cover it up with good deeds, hoping God won't notice. But the light comes on, and there sits our life all crumbled and sorry-looking, covered with half-burned candles and blobs of icing."

"Then what does God do?" Jason asked, sliding slowly into the porch light.

"Why, He loves us so much, He doesn't even notice the mess. He just puts His arms around us and smiles a smile that reaches clear from here to heaven. 'Don't worry,' He says. 'I didn't create you to decorate cakes for Me. I created you to love Me. Don't concern yourself with the mess. Just clean it up and learn from your mistakes. Go on with your life.'"

The old man paused, his eyes searching the boy's tear-moistened face. "It's just a cake, Jason. Nothing more. I know you care about me, not from the job you did, but because you tried hard to please me."

The boy took a timid step forward. "Am I still your friend?"

Professor Appleby fought back tears of his own. "You're my friend forever and ever. Nothing can change that."

Jason ran into the old man's open arms. "Thank you, Professor," he breathed. "Thank you for not being mad. I'll do better next time. I promise."

"Deal!" the old man agreed. "You can be my official cake decorator for as long as I have birthdays." He stumbled to his feet and placed a hand on the boy's shoulder. "Now, how 'bout we go inside and eat that mess on the table?"

"OK!" Jason smiled up at his friend.

"And then I'm going to open my gifts," the professor announced excitedly. "I love gifts. Why, I wish every day were my birthday just so I could get lots of presents from people. My favorite part is unwrapping them." The two made their way up the steps. "I'm not talking about any 'save the paper' unwrapping. No, sir, I rip into those turkeys with a vengeance. I want to see what's inside all that fancy wrapping paper."

Soon the front porch sat silent except for echoes of happy laughter drifting from the kitchen. In the clearing the crickets sang their night songs, unaware that a young heart had learned a valuable lesson about cake decorating, and about a God's undying love for His children.

A CLOSER LOOK

Write That Down, Please

Only a few people in ancient times could read or write. If they wanted to send a message or read a letter or other written document, they had to go to a scribe.

A scribe was a person trained in how to read and write. But he (virtually no women were scribes) was much more than that. He might just copy documents and write up contracts for people, but usually he would also be a government official educated in such subjects as law, business, or economics, with many responsibilities besides reading and writing. The ability to read, write, and do arithmetic in a world in which most people couldn't was a source of great power. A scribe would be what we call today an administrator or bureaucrat.

Scribes preserved society's knowledge and wisdom and acted as counselors to leaders. The book of Proverbs collects many of the wise sayings that ancient scribes taught their students and urged others to follow and live by. Many scribes served as advisers to government leaders and helped to run parts of the government. They were also teachers and educators. Rulers often sent their children to study in scribal schools. Ancient scribes, especially in Egypt, proclaimed that they had the best of all professions.

Many scribes were careful to make sure as few people as possible learned how to read and write. They wanted to protect their position and power in society. Some of the ancient written languages were quite complex, and only a few people could learn them easily. As a result, the scribes who knew how to write had no desire to simplify writing and make it more widespread.

A scribe would use a reed as a brush to write on paper made of papyrus or on animal skins. The ancients used carbon from a burning lamp for black ink and various ground-up mineral pigments for colors. International correspondence often employed clay tablets. The scribe would impress wedge-shaped marks in the soft clay with a wooden stylus. Besides his own language, a scribe might know another language such as Aramaic that many countries employed in diplomatic and business documents.

In Israel during the monarchy the scribe was a high cabinet official involved with finance, policy, and administration. Jeremiah's scribe, Baruch, probably was also a government official, a royal clerk. Baruch may have been the author of the biographical parts of the book of Jeremiah and helped put the rest of the book together for the prophet Jeremiah. Interestingly, archaeologists have found impressions in clay (bullae) of seals that may have belonged to him and his brother Seraiah. Seraiah was minister to King Zedekiah (Jer. 51:59).

Old Testament scribes also held posts in the Temple. Besides copying, reading, and preserving Bible manuscripts, scribes helped teach the meaning of Scripture. After the Exile the Persian king sent the scribe Ezra to instruct and guide the people of Palestine. Many scholars believe that he helped shape the various books of the Old Testament into the form that we have today.

By the time of Christ scribes in the Holy Land had become influential religious officials specially trained in Mosaic law. Sadly, they mostly appear in the Gospels and the book of Acts as His opponents.

But other scribes helped the early Christians spread their faith. The apostle Paul often dictated his Epistles to a scribe. And Christian scribes would copy and preserve the Bible until the invention of printing.

③

Brick by Brick

Stacey, Maria, and Jason sat stone-still on the long, overstuffed couch resting at one end of the big committee room. Miss Baker stood nearby, gazing out the window at the busy college campus below.

Students scurried from building to building, passing each other on the sidewalks, waving, shouting greetings, and checking the time on the large clock above the library. The community college kept a tight schedule of classes. No one wanted to be late.

Across the small campus Miss Baker could see work progressing nicely on the new wing jutting from her own history building—a wing destined to soon become the institution's brand new Appleby-Brewster Museum of Antiquity.

The woman smiled. *How happy the professor and his much-traveled sister will be when the doors to their namesake fly open and guests from across the state, and perhaps from around the world, stop by for a visit.* Of course her students would find much-needed information and inspiration in the artifacts and cultural exhibits planned for the wing.

Miss Baker glanced over at the children. They returned her smile with a degree of uncertainty.

"Now, don't get all nervous on me," she warned good-naturedly. "Dr. Morrison's a kind, understanding man—most of the time. He'll love your idea."

Stacey sighed. "Or he'll think we're crazy. He's done so much for my grandfather already. Now we've cooked up another big scheme. He may just throw us out."

"Well, the parade went off without a hitch—except for the camel thing," Miss Baker replied. The children grinned. "The college is constructing a wing on the history building for the professor and Maggie B's collection of artifacts. I'd say you're doing all right by him."

"But he's the president of the college," Maria stated flatly, "and we're just three kids. He's got more important things to worry about."

"Aren't you forgetting something?" Miss Baker asked. "*I'm* on your side too. So is Stacey's mother, and Mr. McDonald at the radio station. *We're* not kids. So it's six against one. Dr. Morrison doesn't stand a chance."

"A chance for what?" a male voice called from the doorway.

The children turned to see the college president himself striding to the table, a stack of papers in his hands.

"Good morning, Albert," Miss Baker called cheerily. "We were just talking about you."

"Kind comments, I hope."

"Oh, yes. I was telling the children how wise and understanding you are."

The man smiled. "That's what I like about you, Anna," he said. "You're a perfect judge of character." Dr. Morrison sat down and folded his hands over the papers. "Now, what can I do for you folks this lovely autumn afternoon?"

Miss Baker nodded at Stacey, who slowly stood to her feet. "Good morning, Dr. Morrison," the girl said slowly, as if reading from a script. "How are you?"

"I'm fine."

"That's good. I'm glad to hear it. I'm fine too." She cleared her throat. "My friends and I have come here with a request—"

Dr. Morrison lifted his hand. "Stacey, why are you talking like a robot?"

The girl blinked. "What do you mean?"

"It sounds as though you've memorized what you're saying to me."

Stacey blushed. "Well, I sorta wrote down a little presentation, and then sorta memorized it last night. I know how important you are and I'm not very good at talking to important people. They make me sweat and all my spit dries up."

"It's true," Jason called. "You should've seen her when she met the mayor last year. She forgot her own name. Kept calling herself Mrs. Roth's daughter."

"That must be terrible," the man said.

"So," Stacey continued, "that's why I memorized what I

wanted to say. I didn't want to forget anything."

Dr. Morrison waved his hand. "Tell you what. Let's all come and sit here at the table and discuss your idea friend to friend instead of kid to college president. That way I can hear what's on your mind, and you can still swallow. OK?"

The children nodded and hurried to the long conference table. Stacey sat on one side of the college president and Miss Baker on the other. Jason and Maria chose spots across from them.

"Now, isn't this better?" the man asked.

Stacey nodded. "Yes, sir."

"Dr. Morrison," Jason asked, "is it hard being a college president?"

The man smiled. "Sometimes. But when the students are learning and the teachers are teaching, it's the best job in the world." He turned to his young companion. "Now, Stacey— known in some circles as Mrs. Roth's daughter—tell me what's on your mind. And don't bother with your memorized presentation. We're just friends discussing something important to us all."

Stacey grinned. "Thanks, Dr. Morrison. I feel much better now." She pointed at the stack of papers resting in front of them. "Have you read those?"

The man nodded. "Yes, I have. Looked 'em over last night."

"So what do you think?"

Dr. Morrison leaned back in his chair. "Let me get this straight. These are transcripts of the story tapes Maggie B has been sending to Professor Appleby for the past couple years—the same tapes Mr. McDonald has been broadcasting on his radio station?"

"Yes."

"Well, they're very interesting, I must say. The whole town loves her stories. Even Carl, my son. He doesn't miss a single broadcast."

"Right," Stacey nodded. "But you know, the only people who hear these stories are in Valley Springs. Folks in the surrounding cities can't get our station. Mr. McDonald said his signal goes only about 60 miles, then it gets all scratchy and country music from someone else's radio signal covers it up."

"So what's that got to do with me?" the president asked.

"Well," Stacey responded, casting a quick glance at Miss Baker. The woman winked encouragingly. "Your college has something that will help get the stories to more people—even boys and girls all over the world."

"We do?" the man asked.

Stacey nodded. "Yes, sir. It's down in the basement of your industrial arts building. I know. Miss Baker showed it to us."

"Basement of industrial arts?" Dr. Morrison repeated, eyelids lifting. "Why, there's nothing down there except stored building materials, outdated financial records, and an old printing pr—" he paused, mouth stuck in midword. Turning to Miss Baker, he completed his sentence. "Nothing but an old printing press."

The woman grinned. "Bingo!" she answered.

"Wait a minute," Dr. Morrison said, lifting his hand. "You want me to print a book?"

"Oh, no," Stacey chuckled, shaking her head. "You've done so much for us already."

"Whew," the man breathed. "You had me going there for a minute."

"We don't want you to print a book," Stacey laughed. "We want your students to. And it's not one book. It's six. And we'll help."

Dr. Morrison glanced about at his young visitors. "With all the wild notions you children come up with, do you ever have time to sleep?"

"Sure," Stacey grinned. "But when we're awake, we think up neat ideas like the museum and the parade. Now we're thinking about books. Cool, huh?"

The man glanced over at Miss Baker. "And I suppose you're in on this caper?"

"One hundred percent."

Dr. Morrison shook his head. "Aren't you forgetting one small detail?"

"What?" the children asked.

"Money. You know, currency, capital, dollars, funds, green stuff. Just how do you propose to pay for the copy editors, type-setters, artists, press operators—?"

Miss Baker leaned forward. "Student and town volunteers," she whispered as if revealing an exciting secret. "They'll work for free. I'll make it a class project in my department. Martin Parks, chair of the Industrial Arts Department, said he'll donate some of his class time to the process also. Mrs. Roth, Stacey's mother and editor of the town newspaper, said she'll donate enough paper and ink for a small first run. Everything's ready to go. All we need is a printing press."

Dr. Morrison sighed long and deeply. "Why do I get the idea I'm just a spectator and everyone else is making all the decisions?"

"Oh, we would've let you in on it much sooner," Miss Baker said warmly, "but you looked so overworked and undernour-ished. This way all you have to do is say yes and we take care of the rest. We want to keep your life as simple as possible."

The man smiled. "You're all heart. You also get to have all the fun."

"Oh, we plan to involve you," Miss Baker asserted. "There's some legal stuff that needs to be taken care of. A publishing en-tity separate from the college—that kind of thing."

Dr. Morrison clapped his hands in mock glee. "Oh, boy. I get to work with lawyers."

"Maggie B has given her brother power of attorney over her

taped manuscripts," Miss Baker continued. "That means he has the freedom to make decisions for her regarding copyright, distribution of materials, and so forth. Professor Appleby was the one that mentioned that his sister had always dreamed of writing a series of Bible story books for young people." Miss Baker pointed to the stack of papers resting on the table. "Well, now's the time to turn her dream into a reality.

"Professor Appleby wrote a letter some time ago asking me to be his official publishing agent. Maggie B confirmed her wish for a book series and basically gave me the go-ahead to proceed. Neither one has any idea how far we've advanced on this project. We're waiting to surprise them with a finished book, all signed, sealed, and delivered. What we need from you is your support, legal assistance, use of the old college printing press, an OK to utilize volunteer student labor, time on a couple powerful computers, and, of course, a positive word or two delivered in good spirits at your next board meeting."

Dr. Morrison gasped. "That's all?"

Miss Baker smiled. "Yup."

"You sure?" the man asked. "I mean, don't you need my house and car, and perhaps you'd like me to sacrifice my first-born just for good measure?"

"Now, Albert, we're not asking for anything as dramatic as that. Your sweet, understanding, gentle, priceless guidance will suffice." Miss Baker paused. "Unless your car is available for quick trips into the city for supplies. You have a van, don't you?"

Dr. Morrison rolled his eyes. Glancing at the children, he pointed at his faculty member. "See what I have to put up with? And people think being a college president is all speeches and backslapping. Hah!"

Stacey grinned. "So will you help us, Dr. Morrison? You could sell copies of the books right in the museum. It would help raise funds for whatever you want. You're always trying to get money so you can build this or fix that."

The man shook his head. "I'm outnumbered! Now I know how Custer felt at the Little Big Horn." He smiled at his young visitors. "Tell you what I'll do. I'll present this to my board next week at our regular monthly meeting. We'll see what happens, OK?"

"OK!" the children chorused.

"Thanks, Albert," Miss Baker said warmly. "You'll make a lot of deserving people very happy."

"Hey," Dr. Morrison said, rising. "I'm a college president. That's my job, remember?"

With a smile and a wave, he left the room.

Stacey and her companions walked out into the late-afternoon sunlight. The warmth of the autumn sun brushed their faces as they ambled slowly across the campus until they stood before one of the newly constructed walls of the museum wing. Jason picked up a discarded brick and turned it slowly in his hand. "You think they'll do it?" he asked.

Maria flopped down on the grass and pressed her back into the soft carpet of leaves. "Sure they will," she said. "Bible history is just as important as any other kind of history. My mom said this college is supposed to serve the community and help prepare students for life. It makes sense to have these books printed so their graduates can be smarter."

Stacey shook her head. "I don't know. It's not just up to Dr. Morrison. He's got a whole board full of people who may not think it's such a hot idea. They probably will have good reasons, too."

The three sat in silence for a long moment, watching workmen clambering across piles of building materials and shouting instructions to each other. The clock over the library chimed out the message that it was half past the hour. Stacey gasped. "Hey," she said, "it's 4:30." Reaching into her school satchel, she pulled out her small portable radio. "Time for Maggie B. I wonder what hero she'll be talking about today."

The children settled themselves on the ground as Stacey tuned her radio to WPRL, Mr. McDonald's local Christian station. Soon the familiar voice of their faraway friend sounded from the little speaker resting by their heads.

⚒ ⚒ ⚒

Jeremiah bowed his curly head while a long, shuddering sigh shook his body. The news—the shocking news—had left the lonely prophet lonelier still.

King Josiah was dead, killed in battle by Egyptian soldiers. For

31 years he had reigned, but now his crown lay ownerless upon a pillow, and his throne stood empty. Judah had lost what the prophet believed was its finest king. Jeremiah, however, had lost more than a king—he had lost a friend.

In the years since the Lord had called him to be His prophet, Jeremiah had wondered many times why God had chosen him. And now, facing a future without his faithful friend, he wondered again. *I was still a youth when God gave me my first message for the people of Judah*, he remembered. Frightened at delivering a message for God, he had tried to squirm out of the responsibility. "I can't do it!" he had protested. "I'm too young!"

But God had answered, "Before you were born, before you even started to grow inside your mother, I knew you! And I have had plans for you all along. You, Jeremiah, will be a prophet for Me."

Then the most wonderful thing had happened. God Himself had reached out and touched his lips, and the brand-new prophet had heard God saying, "See? I have this day put My words in your mouth. And I have set you over the nations and over the kingdoms, to root out, and to pull down, to destroy, and to throw down, to build, and to plant."

And Jeremiah had done exactly what God told him to do. Embarrassed but determined, he had stood before a crowd of unfriendly Judeans and told them to change their ways. It was the hardest thing he had ever had to do.

But still harder tasks awaited him. God had continued to give him messages, messages that no one wanted to hear. And following God's instructions, he had done all kinds of things to get the people's attention. His face grew warm remembering the time he had paraded through the streets of Jerusalem with a yoke around his neck. "If you do not repent, you will serve your enemies as an ox serves its master," he had warned them.

And because his words were not those they wanted to hear, people threatened him and called him names. They even succeeded in having him imprisoned, his feet and arms locked inside a wooden contraption called stocks. But he still continued to do whatever God commanded. Often he wished, though, that God would leave him alone. Being a prophet was lonely and hard. No one wanted to listen to him.

All I ever wanted was to be a priest, like my father, he thought. *Why did God ask me to be a prophet?*

But it had never occurred to him to say no to God. He loved Him too much for that. Sometimes he felt that God's words burned like a fire in his bones. And while he would much rather have avoided people and kept quiet, he could not. That fire kept him speaking, urging people to turn back to God.

The days after Josiah's death passed swiftly. Then the days became weeks—the weeks, months. One of Josiah's sons, Jehoahaz, now sat on Judah's throne. But after reigning for a mere three months, he fell captive to a band of Egyptian warriors who carried him away to a foreign country.

Soon the people gathered to watch another king crowned. This time Jehoiakim, an older son of Josiah, claimed the throne of Judah. Jehoiakim lost no time in showing the people what kind of king he would be. Wicked to the core, he loved idol worship and reveled in its disgusting ceremonies.

In the fourth year of Jehoiakim's reign God spoke to Jeremiah. "Take a scroll," He directed, "and write upon it all the things I have revealed to you about Israel and Judah and all the other nations. Perhaps when the people hear about the disasters I will soon bring upon them, they will repent of their wickedness. And I will forgive them!"

Jeremiah listened carefully to everything God told him, then he called a scribe, a man named Baruch, to write down everything he had to say. Baruch carefully removed a reed from its little box and dipped it in ink made from charcoal and water. Then he wrote and wrote until he had recorded all that Jeremiah dictated.

The prophet looked it over, nodded his head, then directed, "Go to the Temple. Read these words to all the people as they come in from various towns. Perhaps they will turn from their wicked ways." Baruch wondered for a moment why Jeremiah did not go himself. Then he remembered. Idol-worshiping priests had banned the prophet from entering God's house.

Baruch felt everyone's eyes upon him as he approached the Temple. They knew that he worked with Jeremiah. From various towns all over Judah people had come in honor of a fast day to the Lord. They all worried about the Babylonians. The kingdom of Babylon had grown strong while Judah's old enemies, the Assyrians, had become weaker. Now Babylon threatened to capture them, just as the Assyrians had seized the northern kingdom of Israel.

So the king had proclaimed a fast day. Outwardly the people worshiped the Lord. But they did not honor Him with their hearts. In fact, they wallowed in the wickedness of pagan worship within God's own Temple. The idolaters knew, however, that Baruch never joined in their worship of other gods. They recognized him as Jeremiah's helper, the same Jeremiah whom priests had barred from entering the Temple.

So when Baruch suddenly appeared, a scroll tucked under his arm and a stern expression on his face, the people grew quiet and watched him as he crossed the courtyard.

It was December, and Jerusalem lay cold and damp. Baruch's breath left little puffs of vapor in the air as he climbed to the upper court. Finally he stopped at the New Gate, one of the Temple gates at which important business took place.

In clear, strong tones Baruch read from his scroll. The words burned with the wrath of God, rang with the love of God, echoed with the warnings of God. They told of coming sorrows, of captivity, suffering, and shame. Baruch's message warned Judah— again—to repent. And it warned Jehoiakim, Judah's king, to turn from his evil ways.

A stunned silence followed the reading of the scroll. Then someone exclaimed, "The king must hear this!" The royal officials took a long look at Baruch, then cautioned, "You and Jeremiah had better hide, for the king will want to kill you." They took the scroll from Baruch.

The king, surrounded by members of his court, huddled around a fire in the winter apartment of his palace. He looked up with a scowl as his secretary burst into the room. The secretary ignored the scowl. It meant nothing except that Jehoiakim was in one of his usual bad moods.

"You must hear this," the secretary began, coming right to the point. Edging closer to the king, he began to read Jeremiah's message from God. With each word of reproof, the king's face turned a deeper shade of red. His scowl grew more furious, and his dark eyes snapped with anger.

Suddenly his hand flicked out. In it was his penknife. In a flash he cut off the dangling end of the scroll, the part his secretary had just read. His mouth twisted scornfully as he threw the sacred words of God into the fire.

The flames licked away at the scrap of scroll, sending up puffs of smoke. The secretary gulped, but continued to read. The king's officials stood by, not caring enough about the words of God to even tear their clothes in sorrow or anger.

Again the scroll dangled as the secretary read further along. Again the penknife slashed across the end of it, and the king threw the severed piece of scroll, containing the words of God, onto the fire. As each thought was completed, the king's knife flashed, a shower of sparks flew up as the scroll landed in the burning coals, and the smoke billowed. Just as he would a piece of rubbish, Jehoiakim burned God's words of warning. Finally, as the secretary finished the last word, the defiant king hurled the one remaining stub of scroll into the fire.

But fire could not destroy God's words. Ashes and smoke could not smother them, nor could an ungodly king silence them. God again spoke to Jeremiah. "Write the words once more," He told him. "Write just what you did before. Only this time I'll give you an extra message for Jehoiakim."

Jeremiah obeyed, again dictating God's message while Baruch wrote it down. But at the end of the new scroll appeared God's message to Jehoiakim: "You burned the scroll because it said the king of Babylon would destroy this country and everything in it. But listen to this, Jehoiakim. You will have no heir to sit upon the throne of David. Your dead body will find no burial place, but will be thrown out for the sun to blaze upon by day and the frost to nibble upon at night.

"Because of their sins, your family and officials will also be punished. I will pour out upon them all the evil I promised—upon them and upon all the people of Judah and Jerusalem, for they wouldn't listen to My warnings."

Baruch put down his reed and looked at Jeremiah. The lonely prophet was weeping.

✗ ✗ ✗

WELL, WELL, WELL

Find which well Jeremiah is in by using the clues below. (Answer found on page 118.)

An even number of wells are west of Jeremiah's well.

Jeremiah is not in the well closest to the palace.

Jeremiah's well is further from the sheep than the weaver's well.

Jeremiah is not in a well used for animals' water.

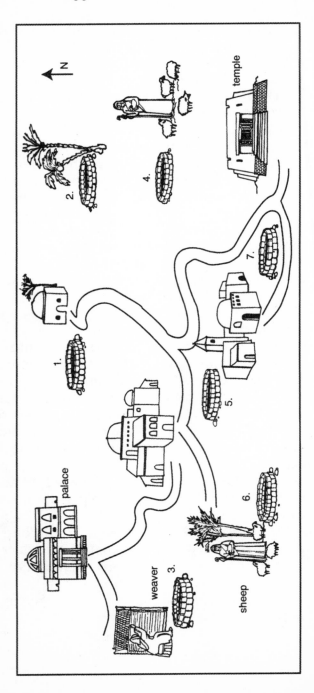

"Wow," Jason gasped as the story ended. "Imagine taking God's words and throwing them in the fire. That was really stupid."

Maria nodded, adjusting her position on the soft, warm carpet of leaves. "My mom said many people just toss away God's words. She says they laugh at what the Bible says and insist it's not important. If it wasn't, why did God tell all those people to write what He wanted to say?"

Stacey watched a workman flip mortar onto a brick and carefully place it on the wall. He tapped one end of the brick until it was level with the rest. Then he reached down and picked up another and repeated the process.

"See that man up there?" she said, pointing at the laborer on the scaffold. "He and the others are putting up a whole wing on Miss Baker's history building. But," she paused, "they don't do it all at once. They build brick by brick, board by board, nail by nail. See?"

Jason and Maria watched for a moment, then nodded.

"Sorta reminds me of something the professor said just last week," the girl continued. "Grandfather said Maggie B wants to help build happy lives for young people. He said she wants to—how did he put it?—place a few pieces of God's love in their hearts. That's why she writes those stories and makes the tapes. She's trying to build something inside of us, something important and strong, like that wall."

Jason turned to his companions. "Her stories are kinda like those bricks. And the book will be like the wall. Is that what you mean?"

Stacey nodded. "Yeah. That's good, Jason. That's exactly what I mean. I'm going to tell the professor what we said. I think he'll like it."

"First let's listen to the next brick—I mean story," Maria giggled. "It's beginning, so turn up the volume, Stacey. Don't want to miss one word!"

Stacey fumbled for the controls just as Maggie B began her adventure.

✗ ✗ ✗

King Zedekiah didn't know it, but he would be the last king of

Judah. Confused and frightened by the demands of the nations around him, he tried to please everyone. Instead he pleased no one, least of all God.

In the morning he joined the sun worshipers who turned their backs to God's holy Temple, bowing to the rising sun. Throughout the day he offered sacrifices to other gods. And in the evening he worshiped the stars.

Jeremiah's voice, mournful and strong, sounded in the streets and in the valleys, from the hilltops and the city gates. "Jerusalem will fall because of its sins! Our only hope of survival is to surrender to Babylon and be taken into captivity. All who remain here will die by the sword. They will die from starvation and from disease."

"That's treason!" the princes and officials exclaimed. "That loudmouthed prophet is saying we should desert our own country in favor of another. Let's tell the king!"

Zedekiah leaned forward, hands on knees, as his court officials reported Jeremiah's words to him. "The man deserves to die!" they exclaimed. "That kind of talk will discourage our soldiers and frighten the people. And he's a false prophet anyway!"

The king stared into the blazing eyes of his advisers. His blood pounded angrily at the thought of Jeremiah's words, and he wanted nothing more than to silence him forever. But something told him that Jeremiah was not a false prophet. He had an uneasy feeling that of all the prophets running around spouting predictions, Jeremiah alone spoke the truth.

What shall I do? he asked himself. God was trying to tell him to listen to Jeremiah. But Zedekiah felt more impressed by the reckless words and blazing eyes of his court officials. "Go ahead," he agreed. "Do what you like with him. I can't stop you."

The officials smirked. Their king could have stopped them. But he lacked the courage to do so.

Jeremiah showed no surprise when a dozen or so of the king's guard marched toward him with ropes in their hands and scowls on their faces. During his years of serving God he had often been treated cruelly. The old prophet took a deep breath. He didn't want to suffer anymore—he didn't want to die. But he knew that whatever he had to go through, God would be with him.

Roughly grabbing him, the men dragged him toward a cistern used to store rainwater in this busy part of the city. At the end of the hot, dry summer, the water in it had dried up, leaving only a pool of mud at the bottom.

And now the sweat popped out on Jeremiah's forehead, little beads of fear. He knew what they intended to do with him. His would be no quick and painless death, but a slow death in a dark hole. His body would cry in vain for water, air, food. And death, when it finally came, would be welcome.

Be with me, Lord! he silently prayed as the men seized each of his arms. Quickly they wrapped a rope across his chest, looped it under his armpits, and tied it behind his back. Then, dragging him to the opening of the cistern, they paused only long enough to shove aside the stone that covered it.

The hole was small, not much bigger around than a large man. It was deep. And it was dark, dark as death.

"Into the hole!" yelled a rough voice, and Jeremiah suddenly felt himself being thrown into the darkness. The ropes bit into his armpits as the men lowered him, down, down, down . . . The light at the top grew smaller. He sensed somehow the space around him getting larger, although he could not see the cistern's sides. But where was the bottom? How far down?

O God, he prayed, *this is the worst yet. Worse than the stocks, worse than beatings, worse than prison. Yet You have cared for me before. So take care of me now!*

Then his feet touched something. Something cold and mucky and slimy. Still he had not reached the bottom of the cistern. He kept falling, those ropes under his arms burning and cutting. The oozing mud swallowed his feet, clung to his ankles, crept up his legs. *Mud!* the prophet thought to himself. *How deep is it? Will I sink in it until it suffocates me?* Already it was above his knees.

Then he stopped. The ropes around him grew slack. The pinpoint of light at the top of the cistern disappeared as someone rolled the stone back over the opening. He heard nothing, saw nothing, felt nothing except the ooze of mud and the creeping dampness that seeped through the pores of his shivering body.

Jeremiah prayed.

Some time later an astonished royal servant listened as palace gossips buzzed about what had been done to Jeremiah the prophet. The servant, Ebed-melech, had himself suffered at the hands of those who held power. Wrenched from his home in faraway Ethiopia, he had become a slave, finally ending up as a court official here in Judah.

Having suffered himself, he felt great pity for the old prophet Jeremiah. Without a thought for his own safety, he rushed to find the king.

"Do you know what your officers have done with Jeremiah?" he demanded when he had located Zedekiah. "The man will surely die from hunger in that disgusting hole!"

Zedekiah, easily influenced by whoever spoke first or loudest, wilted before Ebed-melech's accusing glance. "Uh—I'll see that he's pulled out of there!" he gulped. Then, as a bright idea dawned, "I'll tell you what! You go pull him out yourself. Take three men to help you."

Ebed-melech waited to hear no more. With three young men he dashed into a warehouse and quickly pulled out some rags and old clothes. Then he hurried to the cistern. Would Jeremiah still be alive? Might he have fainted and suffocated in the mud? Could he have died from shock, thirst, weakness, lack of air?

Shoving the covering stone aside, he peered down into the darkness. But he could see nothing. "Jeremiah!" he called.

The prophet glanced up. He could barely spot a face—a kind, black face—staring down at him. "I'm all right!" the prophet shouted.

And he was. God had been with him, strengthening him, comforting him, giving him courage even in his grave of mud.

Quickly tying the rags and clothes together, then lowering them with a rope, Ebed-melech directed, "Stuff the rags and clothes under your arms so the ropes won't hurt you. Then tie the rope around yourself!"

Jeremiah, with cold, trembling fingers, did as he was told. The men began to pull. Jeremiah felt the ropes strain beneath his arms, but thanks to Ebed-melech's thoughtfulness, they did not cut into him or hurt him.

At last, trembling and weak, the prophet sprawled in the sunshine, the light and warmth soothing his body and mind. Silently he thanked God for rescuing him. But out loud he said "Thank you" to the kind Ethiopian, the man God used to rescue His faithful prophet.

✗ ✗ ✗

Maria shivered. "Poor Jeremiah, down there in that awful well. And all that mud! Terrible!"

"Yeah," Jason agreed. "I once locked myself in the basement of our house. Boy, was I scared! I yelled and pounded on the walls until my dad came and got me out. There was no mud, but it was dark and creepy. Sure was glad to see Dad's face looking down at me from the top of the stairs. I got outta there *fast!*"

Stacey sat in deep thought for a long moment. Finally she turned. "Jason, hand me that brick—you know, the one you were looking at."

"It's no good," the boy said. "Gotta chip on one side. The bricklayers threw it away."

"Doesn't matter," Stacey stated. "I've got an idea—something that might help Dr. Morrison."

"Is he building something?" Maria asked.

The blond girl nodded slowly. "Sort of."

Jason handed her the brick. "What're you going to do, throw it through his window with a note that says 'Remember to talk to the board about Maggie B's book'?"

His friend grinned. "Something like that—except I'll leave off the window part."

"What're you up to, Stacey Roth?" Maria queried, a questioning look in her eyes.

Stacey studied the brick in her hands. "Oh, just a little construction work on our wise and wonderful college president. That's all."

④
Building the Wall

S o when do I get my great surprise?" Professor Appleby asked, eyeing his granddaughter expectantly.

Stacey looked up from her homework. "What surprise?"

The old man frowned. "Well . . . ah . . . didn't you and your two cohorts say something about a secret gift in the cards you gave me?"

Stacey tilted her head to one side. "What cards?"

"What do you mean, *what cards?* The ones you gave me for my birthday."

The girl looked blankly at her grandfather. "You had a birthday? Well, I wish you'd told us. We could've had a party or something."

"We did have a party. Right here in this very kitchen." The professor's eyes opened wide. "Don't you remember? There were balloons and streamers, and Jason made a really strange-looking cake, and—" He paused, seeing the grin Stacey was trying hard to hide. "Wait a minute. Wait just a minute. You're foolin' me, aren't you? You're pulling your old, feeble grandfather's leg."

"Now, why would I do such an unladylike thing?"

Professor Appleby stared at the girl for a moment, then tilted back his head and laughed long and loud. "I get it. I get it! You're doing what I do sometimes. Oh, this is rich. This is marvelous! Now I know how you all feel when I have one of my 'lapses,' as I think your mother refers to them. What a hoot! You got me good."

Stacey smiled lovingly. "I wasn't making fun of you, Grandfather. I was just teasing so you'd laugh."

"I know," the old man said between chuckles. "If a fellow can't hee-haw over his own weird ways, then he's a sorry individual for sure. I must really confuse you sometimes with my forgetfulness. Especially when I sometimes pretend to forget something I really didn't."

"Hey, don't worry about it," Stacey said. "I'll set you straight. Mom calls me your guardian angel—the one you can see, that is."

"So," Professor Appleby encouraged, leaning forward in his chair, "how about letting me in on this secret gift? Is it really, really neat?"

"Can't tell you."

"Why not?"

"Just can't."

The old man rubbed his chin. "Is it bigger than a breadbox?"

"Maybe."

"Will it taste good?"

Stacey giggled before she could stop herself. "I don't think so."

"Ah-ha!" the professor shouted. "It's not food. Right?"

"No, Grandfather. I can tell you this much—it's not food."

Professor Appleby bent forward again. "What color is it?"

"Grandfather! I'm trying to do my homework."

The old man's nose scrunched into a scowl. "How can you do homework at a time like this? I have a secret gift that's not food, it's coming who-knows-when, and my very own granddaughter, whom I love and cherish more than anything else in the entire world, knows what it is and won't tell me." His arm shot to his forehead in a dramatic gesture of frustration. "Life is unfair," he moaned, weaving back and forth. "It's a burden on my heart. I think I shall faint dead away and never awaken. Oh, the irony. Oh, the pain."

"Oh, the bad acting," Stacey groaned. "Give me a break, Grandfather. I've been sworn to secrecy." She jumped to her feet. "And wild tigers will not snatch this secret from me. A herd of elephants cannot stomp it from my mouth." She pointed toward the ceiling. "I am a rock of strength, a tower of power, a . . . a . . ."

"A bad actor, just like me," Professor Appleby sighed.

Stacey grinned, returning to her chair. "So I guess we won't be heading for Hollywood anytime soon."

"I've got it," the old man pressed. "You tell me what my surprise is and I'll keep the secret with you. Together we won't tell another living soul even if we're tortured."

"Nope."

"Nothing I can say will change your mind?"

"Nothing."

Professor Appleby thought for a moment. "I'll give you money," he whispered.

"Grandfather!" Stacey gasped.

The old man threw up his hands. "I hate secrets, especially when I'm the one who doesn't know what's going on."

"Then you'll have to be what you're always telling me to be."

"What's that?"

"Patient."

Professor Appleby sighed. "Defeated. I'm defeated. I shall go to my grave a broken and beaten man."

Stacey smiled. "I'll bring lots of flowers."

Thursday morning's pile of mail addressed to Dr. Morrison, community college president, looked the same as it did every Thursday except for the mysterious box covered with brightly colored wrapping paper and postmarked "Valley Springs."

As his secretary plopped the assortment down on his desk, the man looked up sharply. "What's this?" he asked, pointing.

Mrs. Peterson glanced at the pile, then back at her boss. "Your mail. What's it look like to you?"

The man rolled his eyes. "I know it's my mail. I'm talking about the box. What's inside?"

Mrs. Peterson frowned. "Beats me. But if it's ticking, don't open it."

Dr. Morrison grinned. "Now, Mrs. Peterson. You know I don't have any enemies who'd want to blow me up with a mail bomb. Everybody loves me."

The woman paused at the door. "Then you have nothing to worry about. By the way, before you unwrap your mystery box, give me about five minutes to clear the building." With a smile, she closed the door.

Dr. Morrision picked up the parcel and shook it lightly. *Clump.* Something heavy shifted inside. Laying the mystery package down, he began unwrapping it slowly. Finally he gingerly peeked into the dark confines, not sure of what to expect.

"A brick?" he said aloud. "Someone sent me a brick?"

He lifted the object out of the box and held it at arm's length. A neatly folded piece of paper dangled from a string tied tightly around it. "Hey, there's a message attached," he said to himself.

Eagerly the man unfolded the note and held it up to the light streaming through the window behind the desk. The words were carefully penned with elegant swirls and artistic curves. A quick glance at the bottom revealed the writer's name: Stacey Roth.

"Dear Dr. Morrison, I hope you don't mind this unusual gift, but I thought maybe it would teach you the same thing it taught me. Please read this letter before you go to your board meeting. It might give you some ideas for what to say."

The man leaned back in his chair, a curious smile creasing his face.

"I'm only in the sixth grade. I haven't been to college. But I've seen your students walking around the campus and I've heard them talk about school and classes. Guess what? They sound just like me and my friends, except they sometimes talk about older stuff like careers and getting married. They have classes they like and don't like, things they enjoy doing and other things they wish they didn't have to do. Of course, they drive cars. We don't do that yet."

Dr. Morrision chuckled softly to himself.

"But one thing is exactly the same. Students can't learn everything all at once. I mean, it takes years to figure out how to be a doctor (which is what I want to be). Same thing with a businessperson, farmer, plumber, or even a college president like you. Just as it takes a whole lot of bricks to build a building, it takes many, many lessons to learn how to be a good person and help the world.

"Those Maggie B stories can help people learn about history, and about God. They're like small bricks in a big wall. Do you understand what I mean?

"Tell the board members you want to make some learning bricks for your students so they can build a good life for the future. Show them what I sent. I think they'll get the idea.

"And whatever happens, Dr. Morrison, I'm still thankful for your help. You're a nice man, even though you think you're a spectator. Maria, Jason, and I can hardly wait to find out what the board says, so let us know *fast!*

"Your friend, Stacey Roth."

Dr. Morrison laid down the letter and rested his head against the back of his chair. He studied the brick on his desk, its coarse surface etched by the afternoon rays shining through the window. In all the years he'd been a college president, he'd received many requests from well-meaning people. But never had a dream been so clearly spelled out for him. The children of Valley Springs had learned, through the stories of an old woman traveling distant continents, that learning could open up new ways of thinking, new dreams for the future.

What was it about those simple Bible stories? Why had they so affected his town, his college, even his own son?

The man stood and walked to the window. Outside, campus life continued at full tilt. Students rushed by, heads brimming with newfound knowledge, new ideas, new hopes. Why were these stories so important? Why did they have the power to change the very direction of lives? They were just history lessons, right?—no more than ancient accounts of a long-vanished people trying to worship their Creator-God.

And yet the stories of their lives had touched his whole town. Why?

He glanced at the letter once again. Here was a young girl who'd braved her shyness to make her case known. And she'd found in something as simple as a building brick a lesson in learning.

Dr. Morrison's head began to nod slowly. Maybe that was it. Perhaps the value of these Bible stories lay in the fact that they made young people look beyond themselves, to find meaning in the simplest things—even a chipped and discarded building block.

"Mrs. Peterson," the man called, "will you step in here for a minute?"

A smiling face appeared in the doorway.

"How many members do we have on our college board?"

The woman thought for a moment. "Twelve. No, 13."

"Great. Take your student helper, head over to the building site, and bring me 13 bricks."

"Bricks?"

"Yes. You know. As in building-a-wall-type bricks."

Mrs. Peterson paused. "Will you be wanting any mortar with those?"

"No," the man chuckled. "Just get me 13 bricks. I'm going to use them as a visual aid at the board meeting. You'd better hurry. It's almost time."

The woman shrugged and left the office. Dr. Morrison returned to the window, an excited expression lighting his face. "We're going to do it, Stacey," he said softly. "We're going to build something beautiful together."

In the distance the new history building wing was nearing completion. All that remained was some electrical work and the placement of a few more rows of brick.

⚒ ⚒ ⚒

The afternoon sun shone brightly through the leaves surrounding the old mansion in the clearing. All was quiet as Professor Appleby closed the front door and made his way to his favorite spot on the broad porch. The day's museum visitors had departed, leaving the stately old mansion and its sole resident alone by the deep-shadowed forest.

In his left hand the professor carried a tall glass of grape juice, ice tinkling as he walked. His right hand toted a battery-operated radio tuned to his new favorite station—WPRL. It was almost 4:30, and that meant Maggie B's Story Time. Like every other young-at-heart citizen of Valley Springs, Professor Appleby didn't want to miss a single broadcast come hurricane, fire, drought, or World War III.

"Now, Maggie," he said to the radio as he settled his tired body into his patio chair, "you tell a good one today. Course, you tell a good one everyday, but I thought you might like the encouragement."

The old man sighed. "I sure do miss you, little sister. You've been gone away for—what is it now—going on 15 years? Fifteen years! Is that any way to treat the brother who loves you?" Professor Appleby smiled shyly. "A lot has happened since you left; some things I don't even mention in my letters. Too embarrassed." He chuckled. "Imagine me, embarrassed by anything! Well, when it comes to matters of the heart—especially mine— I'm as shy as the next guy."

He placed a hand on the radio. "I've met a lady, Maggie," he

said. "Her name is Anna, Anna Baker. I think you two have cor-
responded concerning the museum.

"She's so kind and thoughtful. Sometimes when I'm with her
I feel like a teenager again—that's right—a silly, fumble-headed
teenager who can't say the right words or do the right things. I
fall all over myself. It's ridiculous. My daughter says she thinks
we're cute together. Cute? No one's called me that since I was 4."

Professor Appleby took a sip from his glass and placed it carefully on the railing. "I always thought love was for the young.
Well, I can see you shaking your head at me and saying, 'Love
never has to go on Social Security. Love *is* social security.' Yup.
That's what you've told me for years and years. I'm just discover-
ing it for myself.

"But I sure do miss you so. I miss hearing your voice, and your
laughter. The story tapes help, but it's not the same.

"Each night before I go to bed, I pray for you, Maggie," the old
man continued. "I ask God to send His angels to hover close to
you as you travel and work in those sometimes violent lands.
Often I fear for your safety. I read news reports and my heart
stands still. Then I remember those angels and feel a little better.

"Just come home someday, Maggie." The man's voice broke
slightly as he spoke. "I want to look into those kind eyes of yours
and hear your laughter. And I want you to meet Anna face-to-
face. You'll fall in love with her just as I have. I know you will."

Reaching over to the table, he turned up the volume on his little radio. "But for now, I'll listen to your story and pretend you're
right here on my porch telling it to me in person. Yes, that's what
I'll do."

As autumn leaves fell silently in the forest, the old man leaned
back in his chair and tried to imagine the caring, time-worn face of
his sister as she spoke directly to him, telling a story from long ago.

❊ ❊ ❊

A tiny stone house, no different from its dozen or more neighbors, clung to a rocky hillside. Outside a couple goats nibbled at
a bush. Wisps of smoke and steam danced lazily above a cooking
pot in the open courtyard.

A woman, looking very much like other women who stirred

their pots for the evening meal, bent over the fire. Her black hair, just sprinkled with gray, hid under a white headcloth. Two deep-set dark eyes lit her weathered face.

But the woman was different from her neighbors, different from most other women in Israel. Elizabeth had no children. Yet she loved God fiercely, joyously, with her whole being. She lived to please Him, still believing that He could bless her with a child. And she lived to see a promise come true—God's promise to send a Messiah to save His people.

Turning, she called her husband's name. "Zechariah!"

A tall, bent form stepped through the door and into the soft light of late afternoon. "Smells good!" he smiled as he sniffed the bubbling stew.

Elizabeth's eyes glowed with pleasure as she hurried to get two pottery bowls. They ate in silence, sitting on goatskin mats around a low table. Again and again they dipped flat pieces of bread into the steaming stew, scooping it into their mouths.

At last Zechariah spoke. "You know that soon it will be my turn to go to Jerusalem to serve as one of the priests at the Temple."

"Yes, I know," Elizabeth nodded. Strange feelings struggled within. She was proud of her husband, proud that he was a priest. But she hated to have him away, even for a little while. Still, he had served many times before, and she knew he would return and life would go on unchanged.

She lifted her chin. "When does your term of service begin?" she asked.

"Next week."

The days passed quickly, too quickly for Elizabeth. Zechariah, too, sighed from time to time. It was a privilege to serve God in the Temple, but he didn't like to leave his wife all alone. *If only we had a son!* he thought, as he had so many times before. Then he chuckled regretfully. What a silly thought at his age!

At last the morning dawned when he would take his donkey and travel the few but rugged miles to Jerusalem. "I'll be home soon!" he promised. He turned to wave just before disappearing over the next hill. Elizabeth waved back, feeling lonely already.

All the way to Jerusalem Zechariah thought and prayed. He talked right out loud to God, with no one around to hear but his long-eared donkey. "It must be time for the Messiah, Lord," he reasoned. "Roman soldiers watch our every move, and the people suffer.

"We've learned some lessons from the past. No longer do we want to worship idols, but Lord . . ." He sighed, finding it hard to put his thoughts into words. "As a nation we're filled with haughtiness and pride. So many of Your priests treat the people as badly as the Romans do, trying to take everything they can away from them, and . . ."

He paused when he could see the walls of Jerusalem below him to the east, high atop a hill, solid as those in the days of David.

During the next several days Zechariah's hands were as busy as his thoughts. Every morning the priests drew lots to see who would perform which duties. Some days Zechariah washed the altar of sacrifice. Sometimes he brought the wood. At other times he burned the offering. As he did, he prayed, "Lord, You've given us this lamb, clean and innocent to remind us that you will send the Messiah. Please send Him soon!"

One morning Zechariah lined up with the other priests. All held up their fingers. Someone shouted a number—"Seventy!" then began counting fingers. Back and forth he walked, counting every finger on the hands of every priest. At last he stopped in front of Zechariah, touching the little finger on his left hand. "Seventy!" he announced.

Zechariah felt a warm, reverent feeling rush over him. The Lord had chosen him to enter the holy place of the Temple and burn incense before the Lord. Already a crowd had gathered—people from Jerusalem, a few from other nearby villages, the old, the young, mothers with babies, children who watched in wide-eyed silence.

Praying silently, Zechariah stepped from the courtyard of the priests into the holy place. The sacred altar of cold, white stone stood in silent splendor. With trembling hands Zechariah raised his censer and sprinkled the incense onto the altar. The strong smell of frankincense and spices filled the room.

He stepped closer to light the fire. But suddenly he cried out. A being—tall, shining, grand, just to the right of the altar—stood watching him with eyes of fire. Zechariah began to tremble.

MYSTERY BABY

Identify who the mystery baby became when he grew up by finding the letters in the shapes given in the clues below. (Answers on page 118.)

_____ ○ + □   _____ ☆ + ◇

_____ ♡   _____ ○

_____ ☆ + □   _____ △

_____ ◇   _____ ✚

                               _____ ♡ + ☆ + □

_____ ✚   _____ ○ + △

_____ ☆ + □   ✚

_____ ☆ + ✚

"Don't be afraid!" the being spoke, the voice as comforting as a mother's lullaby. "Your prayers have been heard, and your wife, Elizabeth, will bear you a son. You are to name him John. He will be a joy and delight to you, and many will rejoice because of his birth, for he will be great in the sight of the Lord.

"He is never to drink wine or anything that could make him drunk, and he will be filled with the Holy Spirit even from birth. He will bring many people in Israel back to the Lord their God.

"And he will do the Lord's work in the spirit and power of Elijah the prophet, to turn the hearts of the fathers to their children, and the disobedient to the wisdom of the righteous—to prepare people for the Lord!"

Zechariah stared. Then he shook his head slowly, as if trying to clear cobwebs from his mind. Was he dreaming, or was it really happening? And *how* could these words be true?

Hesitantly he asked, "How can I be sure of these things? After all, I'm an old man, and my wife is barren!"

The beautiful being smiled, a sad but amused smile. "I am the

angel Gabriel," it announced. "I stand in the presence of God, and He sent me to bring you this news. But because you have not believed my words, and as a further sign that what I say is true, you will not be able to speak until the baby is born!"

Then as suddenly as the angel had appeared, it vanished.

Zechariah staggered toward the door leading to the courtyard. The people looked up with startled eyes. Why had the priest been in the holy place so long? they wondered. Was he all right?

Zechariah opened his mouth to speak, but no words came out. He tried again. Useless. Then he remembered. Gabriel had said he would not be able to speak until his son was born.

Then it struck him—his son—*his son!* A happy smile spread all over his face. Waving his arms wildly, he motioned the people to come near. With gestures, and drawing, and writing on the ground with a stick, he told the amazed people what had just happened.

His next thought was—*Elizabeth!* He must get home to her. Zechariah could hardly wait to see her eyes glow with happiness when she learned that she would give birth to a baby boy, a special child chosen to do a special work for God.

And her eyes did dance and glow when Zechariah, waving his arms, pointing, finally writing, laughing with silent joy, at last managed to tell her the news. Not for a moment did she doubt the words of the angel Gabriel.

Days, weeks, months went by. For five months Elizabeth visited no one, keeping to herself. She hugged herself with joy. The greatest blessing an Israelite woman could know had at last come to her. And every day she thanked God for her own little miracle.

At last she opened her door to her neighbors, and they trooped in, wide-eyed and disbelieving. They shook their heads in wonder at Elizabeth's round abdomen, growing ever rounder with the special baby that developed inside her. Zechariah, unable to speak, beamed from ear to ear.

At last the day arrived when a husky, black-haired baby boy greeted the world with a lusty cry. Eight days later neighbors, relatives, and friends gathered for the special ceremony when the baby would be circumcised and named. Already people thought of the baby as little Zechariah, named after his father.

But Elizabeth heard their whispers and spoke right up. "His name shall be called John!" she declared.

"John?" the people questioned. "Why, no one in your family is called John. That baby should be named after his father!" Excited, they turned to the father, still silent after all this time.

Zechariah picked up a writing tablet. "His name shall be called John," he wrote. "God has picked the baby's name!"

The people gasped. Then they gasped again, for suddenly Zechariah opened his mouth and spoke. "Praise God!" he cried. "Praise the wonderful God who has worked this miracle and given us a son!"

And everyone wondered—what kind of baby was this, whose birth had been announced by an angel, who was born to a barren couple, who had been named by God Himself?

But little John snuggled close to his beaming mother and slept. She knew that this sleeping baby was not like other babies. Some day he would awaken everyone with a message from God.

⚔ ⚔ ⚔

Professor Appleby shifted his position as the announcer cued up the next tape. "What happened to this tiny baby?" the old man asked his unseen sister. Then his smile faded. "I already know. I've read the account in the Bible. But the children of Valley Springs need to learn just how far Satan will go to silence one of God's messengers."

He sighed as the adventure continued.

⚔ ⚔ ⚔

Dark-skinned slave girls with swinging black hair weaved and danced in time to the music. Their graceful motions flowed across the floor of marble pieces inlaid in geometric patterns. Inside the palace a circle of men watched the dancing girls. And Herod, relaxing on cushions, leaned forward, his head full of music, enjoying every movement.

Unknown to him, someone else eagerly watched the performance. Salome, his wife's daughter, peeked around the corner, observing every gesture. Her own body swayed as she watched. And she thought, *I wish I could dance in public! But I'm a princess, so it's not permitted. Everyone would say I'd disgraced myself!* Her lower lip pouted and a frown creased her smooth young forehead.

At last the dance ended. The slave girls dropped to the floor, faces down, arms extended. Then leaping to their feet, they seemed to simply disappear into the walls. The musicians picked up their instruments and left.

But Salome lingered. Catching a glimpse of herself in a polished bronze shield hanging on the wall, she smiled at herself, bending low. Then, the persistent rhythms of the dance echoing in her head, she began to imitate the intricate motions of the slave girls.

Weaving, turning, stepping high, bowing low, she flirted with her own image. Growing bolder, she tossed her head so that her long black hair swung out behind her. Her cheeks flamed with excitement, and her soot-black eyes sparkled as she danced faster and faster.

Suddenly she stopped, nervous and confused. She felt, rather than saw, that someone was watching her. Turning, she stared straight into Herod's eyes. The look in them showed that he was impressed, and that made her blush out of pleasure.

Abruptly she turned and walked away, smiling to herself, aware that Herod's eyes followed her every movement.

Herodias, Herod's wife and Salome's mother, had witnessed the whole incident. *So,* she thought to herself, *my husband's roving eye has noticed Salome. Well, well. Who knows? Perhaps that bit of information might someday prove useful to me.*

Long months had passed since she had badgered Herod into imprisoning John, the prophet who had baptized people at the Jordan. But her determination to see John dead had never faltered.

During all this time John had huddled in his prison cell, chained in the chilly darkness. A thousand questions tormented his mind. Why was he here? And why did not his cousin Jesus send him some word of encouragement?

His own disciples visited faithfully, bringing him food and news of Jesus. John knew he would never forget the day he had baptized his cousin as a voice from heaven thundered, "THIS IS MY BELOVED SON, IN WHOM I AM WELL PLEASED!"

But the news his disciples brought only stirred up more questions, more doubts. If Jesus was the Messiah, why had He not taken some action to overthrow Roman power and set God's people free? And why didn't everyone bow in deep repentance from sin in His presence? John shook his shaggy head, trying vainly to find answers to his questions.

One day as his disciples visited him, they told how Jesus sat down and ate with tax collectors and sinners. They mentioned that the Jewish leaders said His power to work miracles came from the devil. Even His own family, they confided, did not support His work.

John's head drooped lower. In his inmost soul he knew that Jesus was the Messiah. But the terrible doubts persisted. *If Jesus was the Messiah, why didn't He act like Israel's strong deliverer?* And the frightening thought stabbed his consciousness—had he given his whole life to the wrong cause?

He had to have some kind of answer. "Please," he begged, looking up at his friends with anguished eyes, "go to Jesus and ask Him if He is the promised one, or if we should look for another."

The words burned like poison on his lips. He felt ashamed for voicing his doubts, but he needed reassurance. And he needed it badly.

So one day as Jesus attended to the needs of a huge crowd, He noticed two of John's disciples approaching Him. They had doubt written all over their faces.

He felt pity for the troubled men. But most of all His heart went out to John himself. Yet He knew that John, through his brave suffering in prison, would persuade more people to love God than he ever could if he were free to continue his powerful preaching.

John's disciples edged closer to Jesus. As soon as He could turn His attention from the crowd to them, they asked, "Are you the one who was promised, or should we look for another?"

A shadow darkened Jesus' eyes—a shadow of pain and sadness. So even John doubted Him. John, who at the river Jordan had seen God's presence and heard His voice proclaiming Jesus to be His own Son. If John doubted Him, who would believe?

But He quickly shook off such thoughts. John, like others, simply did not understand His purpose or His methods. He gazed silently for a moment at the waiting disciples. Then, without a word, He turned back to the crowd.

The lame, blind, fevered, and fainting pressed around Him. Some were so sick they had to be carried. People possessed by devils threw themselves at His feet.

At His touch, His word, the dying, now bursting with health, rose from their beds. The lame, on two strong legs, jumped for joy. The blind gazed into the loving eyes of Jesus and praised Him for the gift of sight. The calm light of reason replaced the mad glare of the devil-possessed. Wherever Jesus turned, health, joy, and praise to God sprang up like spring flowers after the winter rains.

Hours passed. Still the people came. Jesus never turned anyone away. And as He healed suffering bodies, He spoke words of encouragement, forgiveness, and comfort to their troubled minds. John's disciples watched, open-mouthed, at the demonstration of God's love.

At the end of the day Jesus finally turned to them. "Go and tell John what you have seen and heard," He said softly.

The very next day, as John huddled in his cell, fighting his fears and his doubts, his disciples came to him. Breathless with excitement, they told in hurried bits and pieces of Jesus' wonderful works. They described the crowds who arrived hopeless and miserable, only to leave joyously praising God. And they spoke of Jesus' love, reaching out to everyone, no matter how deformed by disease, no matter how wicked or despised.

Tears glistened in John's eyes as he listened. A text from Isaiah suddenly sang in his heart: "*The spirit of the Lord is upon me . . . to preach good news to the poor, to bind up the brokenhearted, to set the captives free. He has anointed me to proclaim the year of the Lord's favor and comfort all who mourn.*"

"It's Jesus!" he cried excitedly to His disciples. "The text in Isaiah—it's talking about Jesus! He *is* the Messiah!" From that moment on he trusted Jesus completely, accepting even those things he did not understand. Never again did he doubt.

But Herod had his doubts—about John. Plenty of them. He doubted that he should ever have sent such a good man, a prophet no less, to prison. *Some day I'm going to free him!* he promised himself. But every time he thought of the wrath of Herodias, he lost his courage.

But she never allowed doubt or guilt to trouble her. Glad that John was in prison, she hated him for publicly calling her a sinner. Day and night her mind wrestled with the question *How can I convince Herod to put him to death?*

Then an opportunity presented itself. Herod would soon celebrate his birthday. He had invited lots of friends to his party. They would hold the celebration at his mountain castle, away from the heat of the valley.

That's where that John the baptizer is imprisoned! Herodias told herself with a wicked thrill of anticipation. Carefully, saying nothing to anyone, she laid her plans.

The night of the big party arrived. Visions of John, chained in the dungeon below, haunted Herod. In a frantic effort to drown his fears, he poured cup after cup of wine down his throat. His friends eagerly joined him. The music and dancing became more frenzied. And Herod and his friends grew more drunk.

Herodias and Salome watched the wild party from a hallway.

The older woman's eyes narrowed, her heart hammering with revenge. The time was almost right. She wanted Herod drunk, but not so drunk he couldn't do what she wanted.

Suddenly she whispered "Now!" and pushed Salome into the banquet hall.

The king's eyes started from his head. His drunken guests stared in amazement. *The princess! The princess had come to dance for them!* Their muddled minds didn't know whether to be embarrassed for the beautiful Salome, or flattered at the unheard-of honor to themselves.

Then Salome began to dance. Using all the tricks she had learned from the slave girls, and a few that her mother had taught her, she gave herself up to the rhythm of the music. And Salome danced as no one had ever danced before, a toy of the music, nearly dizzy with power as she charmed every man in the room.

Her heart pounded with the exertion. Her cheeks glowed. A mist of sweat glistened on her smooth skin. She picked up the pace of the dance, moving faster, faster.

At last she finished, facedown on the stone floor. In one hand she held a filmy veil.

Herod leaped to his feet, swaying drunkenly. His bleary eyes glittered. "Name your heart's desire!" he shouted to Salome. "I swear by my throne, you may have whatever you want, even to half the kingdom!"

Salome's eyes flashed in triumph. Everything was happening just as her mother had predicted. She had played her part well.

Dashing into the hallway, she met Herodias, beside herself with excitement. "What shall I ask for?" Salome whispered.

Herodias hissed her answer. "The head of John the baptizer on a silver platter!"

The blood drained from Salome's face. Was *this* why she had danced? Was *this* what her vanity had accomplished? Was *this* her mother's evil purpose? Horror-struck, she whispered, "I danced a dance of death!"

But Herodias's eyes held no pity. Bold, hard, and triumphant, they gripped Salome in their spell. "Now go!"

As if sleepwalking, Salome returned to the banquet hall. Lifting her eyes to Herod's face, she whispered, "Bring me the head of John the baptizer on a silver platter!"

Herod fell back as if struck with death. His flushed face turned pale, his eyes held a tortured, cornered look. He wanted to take back that promise.

But his drunken friends laughed mercilessly. "She wants the head of the pesky prophet! Well, a promise is a promise, old boy, and you swore by your throne!"

Through wooden lips Herod gave the order. And minutes later John the baptizer lost his life.

In the days to come Herod had terrible dreams. He began to hear more and more stories about Jesus, the miracle worker. And he wondered superstitiously if Jesus were really John the baptizer, come back to haunt him. The ruler never knew another day of rest, another night of peace.

When Jesus heard the news of John's death, he bowed His head in sorrow. At last He lifted His tear-filled gaze to His friends, and proclaimed, "Never, among all men born, has there been one greater than John the baptizer!"

✘ ✘ ✘

Professor Appleby shook his head slowly from side to side. "That's a sad story," he said to himself. "But God sent another messenger, then another, and another. He always does."

The man glanced at the radio and switched it off. "That's what you are, Maggie. You're a messenger, telling the people of Valley Springs of God's love. And if anyone offers to dance for you, tell them you like your head right where it is—on top of your shoulders."

He stood and walked across the porch. "It's getting kinda cold, Maggie," he said. "Winter's just around the corner." He gazed into the forest. "I wish you were here with me to watch the leaves fall."

Slowly he turned and entered his old Victorian home, closing the door behind him.

WORD SEARCH—PLACES

Find the hidden words in the puzzle below. They will read horizontally, vertically, or diagonally—frontward or backward. The names you need to find are listed below the puzzle grid. (Answers on page 118.)

```
L O Q A T D V G L U G P D P H H A W S C
O I L H G F K V W F F O T B G P U R L A
A E T Q A N F O R H B M M Q W H Y F B H
G G N L L Z A E T X N L K O H D N Q V C
N I E T R Q O E O E X J V G R A J G A E
U V Y B N T R R Y H D N N R C R L V F A
D N V R P A I Y B G C W Z O O S A D K N
C C W D Z N N A W L A I Y S K S A H Q K
R U H A G M I R L M B P R F Z H B D A S
G Q N B L P E D N E A H E E Z J M P I S
G J N F O U H G O L B E B D J S M H H O
Q D J I B W K P L A Y B W G F L A U P L
A X H U N R N M G S L R M H D E J R A Y
E T G J O E F L E U O O P E R L E U J Y
E V A C E T A O M R N N F T L J R V Q H
P C L P B J D U S E X D X U S A F P A L
B U I S I J Z Q V J Q I R R G U S X P O
U R L R G D K E Z Z K E G Y P T H T D F
L E E S K U P Z E F C X Z K B P R H U E
G X E A M O D O S A N J T E Q P K J V M
```

Babylon	Ethiopia	Gomorrah	Japhia	Nazareth
Eglon	Galilee	Hazor	Jericho	Salem
Egypt	Gibeon	Hebron	Jerusalem	Sodom

⑤
Clunks and Rattles

T he first snows of winter swirled and danced across the college campus like ivory butterflies. Christmas was still four weeks away, but already the interior walls and windows of each building boasted colorful reminders of the joyous season to come.

The school had been the center of much activity during the past few months with truckload after truckload of boxes brimming with artifacts and souvenirs arriving at the back door of the new history wing—most from Professor Appleby's mansion museum, and others coming directly from Maggie B. Miss Baker's face seemed to smile more every day as she watched the museum fill with mysterious and unusual objects.

With willing students at her side she created displays, painted walls, labeled information cards, and cataloged each valuable item entrusted to her care.

Another reason for her growing smile arrived daily at 9:00 a.m. sharp, rubbing his hands together in eager anticipation of the day's labors. Together Professors Appleby and Baker would roll up their sleeves and attack the latest collection of artifacts, creating eye-catching displays and detailed written records for their library.

Now that they were an official, registered museum of antiquity, items previously withheld by foreign governments could be sent for display. Even before all the exhibits were completed, students strolling into the large presentation hall felt as if they were traveling back through the centuries to a time long vanished and, for most people, forgotten. That was precisely the effect the two hardworking curators wanted to achieve.

Stacey, Maria, and Jason had been busy too, except they wouldn't tell anyone what they were up to. Occasionally Professor Appleby would see his granddaughter emerging from the industrial arts building with her young companions. The old man would call out and wave. The children would return his greeting, giggle among themselves, then run away—very uncharacteristic even for those three.

The professor figured they were up to some secret mission he'd find out about eventually. At least they were hanging around a college campus instead of getting into trouble in town.

"I wonder what they're up to," the old man said one afternoon after a chance run-in with his granddaughter and her two friends. He and Miss Baker were hard at work in the museum, his portable radio playing softly in the background. "Whatever it is, they sure giggle a lot."

Miss Baker looked up from the ceremonial bronze shield she was carefully polishing. Inlaid with red glass, more than likely it had been the proud possession of a Roman officer.

"Kids. Don't try to figure them out. They live in a world all their own." She shot a quick glance at her companion, then looked back at her work. "They probably have some project under way they don't want anyone to know about."

Professor Appleby nodded. "Whatever it is, it sure makes them happy. They're over in the industrial arts building almost every afternoon. Maybe I should stop by and see wh—"

"No!" Miss Baker delivered the word with more force than she'd planned. "I mean, maybe that's not a good idea. They could be working on a Christmas present for someone we know. Wouldn't want to spoil the surprise, would we?"

The professor tilted his head slightly. "No. We wouldn't want to do that."

Miss Baker rolled her eyes. "Now, don't be getting any big ideas in that old, worn-out brain of yours. You just let those children be. Let them finish doing whatever they're doing in peace."

"It doesn't matter," Professor Appleby sighed. "I already know what's going on."

Miss Baker's hand paused over the shield. "You do?"

"Yup. They're building me a new bed frame. Mine's been broken for quite some time now. Stacey saw it about a month ago when she was helping me vacuum. Said it was a shame I had to sleep on a broken frame and that I should get a new one. I told her I didn't mind sleeping downhill—keeps a fresh supply of blood around my brain. I don't think she believed me, so they're over there building me a new one. Yes, sir. That's what those kids are up to."

"You may be right," Miss Baker smiled, a hint of relief in her voice. "So just let 'em be."

"You bet I will. I don't mind saying I'm tired of dreaming someone is pushing me off a cliff. That never happened when I was lying flat."

Miss Baker grinned over at her companion. "So promise me you won't go snooping around the industrial arts building, OK?"

"OK," the professor replied. "But I hope they hurry. It's cold in that big house. With that silly bed, winters can be pretty tough."

"Why?"

The old man lifted his hands. "Covers keep rolling off. I wake up shivering like an aspen leaf and find all the blankets piled around my neck."

Miss Baker burst out laughing. "Well, you crazy old codger. Why don't you take the mattress and box springs off the frame and put them flat on the floor? Then nothing will slide off, summer or winter."

Professor Appleby thought for a minute. "Then how will all that fresh blood get to my brain?"

The woman shook her head slowly. "I give up. You're impossible!"

"I just need someone to take care of me," the professor said shyly. "Someone to help me keep my blankets straight."

Miss Baker blushed. "Well, just maybe that's the best idea yet."

"It's 4:30," a voice on the radio interrupted, "and time for Maggie B. So drop what you're doing, kick off your shoes, and relax as our friend from faraway introduces us to more Bible heroes."

Professor Appleby smiled over at his companion. "We'll continue this conversation later. OK?"

Miss Baker nodded, her eyes filled with admiration for the gentle man sitting beside her. "OK," she said. "But soon. Winter's here."

As snowflakes fell beyond the windowpanes, Maggie B's voice filled the presentation hall and carried her listeners to a land far beyond the horizon surrounding Valley Springs.

✗ ✗ ✗

Jews from far-flung lands and foreign cities poured into

Jerusalem. In a time-honored ceremony a priest stood before the Temple altar and offered a sheaf of barley, the first of the harvest, to God. The courts rang with happy voices and the steady drone of prayer while smoke from burning sacrifices wafted toward the sky.

On this ceremonial Sabbath they had come to celebrate the festival of grain harvest. For centuries people had called it the Feast of Weeks or the Feast of Firstfruits. Now many referred to the special day by a Greek word, Pentecost. But no matter what people called it, it was a time of joy and thanksgiving.

Among those gathered in Jerusalem were Jesus' disciples. Ever since He had ascended to heaven, they had remained there according to His instructions. "I will send the Holy Ghost upon you," He had promised. So now they waited. But they did more than simply wait. They prayed and talked about their Lord, trying to remember everything He had ever said or done while they had been with Him.

"I wish we had understood more of what He told us!" they exclaimed again and again. "Why didn't we realize right away that He was the Messiah? Why didn't we grasp the lessons He tried to teach us, or comprehend that He would die for the sins of all people? We must have disappointed Him so many times when we failed to understand His words." The conversation went on and on, sometimes happy, sometimes sad, but always full of hope.

Jesus had given them that hope, for He had promised to send them a Comforter, the Holy Spirit. They told others of their new hope, constantly assuring all who would listen that Jesus of Nazareth had come as their Messiah. "And He rose from the dead!" they exclaimed excitedly. "We saw Him rise up into the sky. We saw the angels take Him back to heaven. But He has promised to return for all who will accept Him as their Saviour from sin!"

Now on this ceremonial Sabbath, as they met together in a dimly lit room near the Temple, they continued to pray, confessing their sins and pleading for the Holy Spirit. James and John no longer worried about who would be the greatest in God's kingdom. Peter finally understood what it meant to love others as Jesus did. And not one of them gave in to a selfish thought or even considered indulging in a petty quarrel.

Outside hummed the sounds of the city. The deep droning of men in prayer, the softer, higher-pitched tones of the women, the light, bright voices of the children, all mingled with the bleat of animals and the air-splitting blast of a ram's horn.

Suddenly a sound like no other filled the room where the disciples were praying. Like a rushing, mighty wind it swept through the group. It roared like a tempest; then seemed to burst into visible flame. Each disciple cried out in astonishment as he saw the flames separate and settle on every one of them like tongues of fire.

Then—to their own amazement—they began to speak in foreign languages. A babble of voices filled the room. At last all fell silent, as the wonder of what was happening slowly dawned on them.

Their prayers had been answered! Jesus' promise had been fulfilled! And the Holy Ghost had come to them with all the power of heaven.

Compelled by the divine power, they rushed into the Temple courts, where godly Jews from many nations had come to celebrate and thank the Lord for His blessings. But the visitors had never dreamed of the blessing God had in store for them now.

Peter began to preach. Jews from the island of Crete listened, astonished, as they heard him perfectly pronouncing the words of their own language. John spoke to the people of Cappadocia. And they understood each syllable. James spoke in the language of those from Egypt. Their faces aglow with their love for Jesus, the disciples preached clearly, powerfully, while the crowds gathered around them.

Struck by the truth of the disciples' words, the listeners believed Jesus' promise that He would return and take them home to heaven with Him. But their amazement at the disciples' skill in their own languages knew no bounds.

The news spread—"These men are simple fellows from Galilee!" The people of Jerusalem considered Galileans backward and uncultured.

"Then how did they ever learn such perfect Greek? How did they learn Arabic or the Egyptian language? They speak our languages better than we do!"

But they soon understood that God is a God of miracles, the

Creator of life and lands and languages. And He had sent the Holy Spirit at just the right time, to just the right place, so that thousands could hear about His crucified and risen Son.

Peter's voice soared above the crowd. "Repent and be baptized, every one of you. Do it in the name of Jesus Christ, that your sins may be forgiven. And you too will receive the gift of the Holy Spirit. The promise is for you and your children, and for everyone, near or far."

Fathers and mothers with their boys and girls did just as Peter urged them to do. By the scores they came. By the hundreds they were baptized.

When that day of Pentecost finally ended, about 3,000 people had been baptized. God had answered the disciples' prayers in a most amazing way. The Holy Spirit had come. Jesus had kept His promise, just as He always does.

✕ ✕ ✕

Mr. McDonald slid the volume control knob of his microphone up a few inches and leaned forward slightly. "Just a reminder to all my Maggie B listeners," he said, watching the voice meter move with his words. "Keep a week from this Sunday free on your calendar, because that's the day our brand-new Appleby-Brewster Museum of Antiquity officially opens on the campus of the community college. Dr. Morrison, the president, reports lots of activities scheduled with fun for young and old alike. Who knows, maybe there'll even be some surprises in store. Open house begins at 1:00 p.m., so do plan to be there and show your support for our college and the new museum. I'll be reminding you again in the days to come. It's an important event for the citizens of Valley Springs. Mark it on your calendar.

"And here again is the woman who inspired it all, Maggie B."

✕ ✕ ✕

He had been born crippled. His mother had turned her face away from him and cried when she first laid eyes on his twisted feet and ankles. His father had rushed off to the Temple, begging God to forgive him for whatever sin he had committed. *Surely,* he reasoned, *I must have done something bad to have God curse me with a crippled son.*

Eventually his parents named him Eliku, meaning, God has spit him out. But God had not spit out this baby boy or cursed him. His crippled feet were only an accident, not a punishment from God.

Still, Eliku grew up feeling as if God were scowling at him. Certainly everyone else was! His father's bushy eyebrows met in a black frown every time he looked at him. His sisters and brothers ignored him, pretending that he wasn't truly a part of their family. People he didn't even know tried not to look at him, and when they did, their eyes held no kindness. He suspected that his mother might love him, but she felt so guilty about having given birth to a cripple that she touched him only when necessary.

The years passed in a blur of loneliness—and pain. His crippled feet and ankles often hurt, and many times he wondered why he had been born at all. As his body changed and grew, the bones in his legs lengthened, but his feet remained shrunken and twisted. The muscles in his legs trembled with weakness as they dangled from his frail body.

Eventually he became a man. His parents grew old and died. Knowing that it was their duty to care for him, his brothers and sisters made sure that someone carried him each day to a place where people gathered, usually at one of the Temple gates. There they left him—to hold out his hand and beg.

More years went by. Eliku, with other beggars, watched the people gather as they came to worship at the Temple. He listened to every bit of news that came his way. The begger heard lots of talk about sin and God and the law. One great teacher after another discussed this subject or that.

And he heard talk about Jesus. Strangely, he had never seen Him, even though the great Teacher and Healer had visited the Temple many times. *Wish I could have met Him before He died,* Eliku often thought. *People say He healed cripples. I wonder if He could have healed Me—or if He even would have wanted to.*

But now, of course, it was too late. Roman soldiers had crucified the kind Miracle Worker. Some said that He had been resurrected, that His disciples had seen Him ascend to heaven, and Eliku felt inclined to believe it was true. But Jesus was no longer around, and any chance he might have had for healing had vanished with Him.

On a chilly fall afternoon Eliku's helpers carried him once again to the Temple. It was almost time for the evening prayers, and many climbed the hill toward their beautiful place of worship. Already people thronged its courts and gates. Other beggars crowded the gates, hands outstretched, hoping someone would be generous enough to drop a coin into them.

"Take me to the Gate Beautiful," Eliku suddenly directed, not quite sure why he had chosen that one when others were just as busy and easier to reach.

The gate he had selected was indeed beautiful. Made of solid Corinthian brass, it outshone the other nine outer gates overlaid with gold and silver. Heavy and costly, it took 20 men just to close it.

Carelessly his helpers dropped him on his mat and hurried away. Eliku's hopeless eyes scanned the familiar scene—other beggars, heedless crowds, the massive, gleaming Temple. And he wondered what this day had in store. Would someone be extra-generous this afternoon? Would he leave at the end of the day with enough coins to buy a good supply of bread, maybe even some dates or honey? Or would the crowd hurry past him, not wanting to look upon a cripple? He sighed, wondering again why God had cursed him.

Then he spotted two men coming toward him. Something about them seemed to say, *We care about people. You can talk to us.*

One was a big, bushy-bearded chap. Everything about him seemed to be in motion. His legs covered the ground in long, impatient strides. His huge arms swung recklessly. And he talked eagerly to his companion, jerking his head every now and then to punctuate a sentence.

The other man looked somewhat younger. A kind of gentleness clung to him, quite unlike anything Eliku had seen before. Even when his face was serious, his mouth seemed always ready to smile. His dark eyes glowed and twinkled as he listened to his older companion.

Suddenly the two were right in front of him. *I feel sure these men will give me some money,* Eliku thought. He stuck out his hand. "Please, some coins for a beggar?" he implored.

Peter stopped talking, while his eyes filled with compassion.

John turned a sympathetic gaze on the man whose shriveled, twisted feet had doomed him to a hopeless life. Both of Jesus' disciples could see the pain in Eliku's eyes. And they knew that it did not come alone from his crippled ankles and feet. They saw the pain of loneliness, the misery of a life lived without love.

Peter broke the brief silence. "Look at us!" he commanded, his tone full of urgency. Eliku gave them his full attention, expecting a donation at any moment.

But Peter had a surprise for him. "I don't have any silver or gold," he said, and the crippled man's heart sank.

"But what I do have, I give to you. In the name of Jesus Christ of Nazareth—*walk!*"

That *name* . . . the name of Jesus . . . that *power* . . . the power of Jesus!

In an instant Eliku sprang to his feet, grasping Peter's outstretched hand. Strength flowed into his ankle bones. His muscles felt firm and fit as his feet—his beautiful, straight feet—stood

securely on the ground. But not for long. Soon those feet leaped into the air. They danced, finally settling down to a joyful walk.

And all the while he shouted, "Praise God, I've been healed! In the name of Jesus of Nazareth, I've been healed! Praise His name—now I know that God loves me!"

Peter and John both wore splendid smiles as they walked with Eliku into the Temple. "Thank You, Jesus!" they whispered, thrilled that even though they could not see their beloved Master, He was still with them, working miracles.

The sight of a former cripple leaping through the Temple court-yard caused a great commotion. "Isn't that the beggar, the one crippled since birth?" the people asked one another in astonishment.

"Yes, it is! But how could he possibly be walking? He's never walked before in his whole life!"

"Those men, Peter and John, healed him through the name of the One who was crucified, Jesus of Nazareth!"

The Jewish leaders were alarmed, frustrated, furious. Would they never silence Jesus' followers? Would they never stop hearing that name?

Then Peter, who once had been too cowardly to admit that he even knew Jesus, saw the people's interest and stood up and preached to all that great crowd. And he preached the name of Jesus—Jesus the Son of God, whose power is great enough to forgive sins, to heal the crippled, to overcome death itself.

Eliku's eyes shone. *I love Jesus!* he thought to himself. *I can hardly wait for Him to come again, as He promised He would. And when I see Him, I'll run to Him on my straight, strong feet and thank Him for healing me and changing my life!*

༒ ༒ ༒

As the story ended, Stacey walked to the far side of the crowded room and glanced out the window. In the background the steady *chi-conk, chi-conk, chi-conk* of a machine shook the basement floor. "Snow's getting kinda deep," she called excitedly. "I think we'll be dusting off our sleds tonight. I can hardly wait."

"Yeah!" Jason called, his hands and arms stained with dark smudges. "Maybe we can even get your grandfather to go sledding with us. Remember the last time he did? It was fun."

Maria peeked from behind moving machinery, each part keeping time to a persistent melody of rattles and clunks. She pointed a long-necked oil can at the window. "Maybe it's a blizzard."

"Nah," Stacey responded, shaking her head sadly. "Just a big snowfall. We'll have school tomorrow. You can count on it."

The radio blasting from the shelf above their heads announced the next Maggie B story. With one ear tuned to the voice speaking above the din, the children returned to help the college students and their instructor with their work.

✕ ✕ ✕

A huge crowd had gathered around Peter and John and the beaming man who had lived all his 40 years as a cripple. Scarcely believing their own eyes, they stared at Eliku, standing strong and straight and healthy. His face shone with gratitude to Peter and John and the God who had healed him.

John stood boldly by Peter's side, while the bushy-bearded ex-fisherman preached in the Temple courts. "Even Moses, whom you honor, said, 'The Lord your God will raise up for you a prophet like me from among your own people; you must listen to everything he tells you.' Indeed, all the prophets from Samuel on have foretold these days.

"God told Abraham, 'Through your offspring all peoples on earth will be blessed.' And when God did raise up His Servant, Jesus of Nazareth, He sent Him first to you to bless you by turning you from your wicked ways."

The people listened, clinging to every word Peter uttered. His message rang with truth. And there—right there at Peter's elbow—stood a miracle, the man who had been crippled from birth.

The crowd swelled as more and more people swarmed into the huge Temple court. Exclamations of "Praise God!" rippled through the throng. Soon the priests and the governor of the Temple heard the commotion in the outer courts. Puffed up like crows on a cold day, they sailed into the crowd to confront the two disciples of Jesus.

"What right do you have to speak here?" they demanded, outraged that a couple unschooled fishermen should take it upon themselves to preach in the very courts of the Temple. "You have no authority to speak here!"

The Sadducees were especially upset. They did not believe in the doctrine of the resurrection. Yet here in front of them were two of Jesus' disciples, claiming that He had risen from the dead. What's more, they had performed a miracle in His name, and now thousands of people were listening to them, marveling at the healed cripple and believing in Jesus—and the resurrection.

"Arrest him!" they hissed to the Temple governor. As the one responsible for keeping order in and around the Temple, he quickly gave the command.

Roughly grabbing Peter and John, the Temple police whisked them away from the crowd of sympathetic people. The priests and Sadducees could hardly wait to hold a trial and pronounce punishment on the two disciples, but a glance at the sky told them they would have to wait.

The blushing sun shimmered on the horizon, eager to hide itself under a blanket of night. And that meant that they would have to postpone the trial of Peter and John until morning, for it was against Jewish law to conduct a trial at night.

Peter and John exchanged sober glances as the guards hurried them toward a public building with an underground room used for holding prisoners. Jesus had warned them that they would be persecuted for believing on Him. Now the persecution had begun.

They felt uneasy, wondering what would happen next. But not for a moment did they consider taking back their words. They would never apologize for talking about their wonderful Jesus. They loved Him too much for that.

Then they were being shoved into a cold, dark room. A foul odor slapped their nostrils. The guards clamped iron chains around their wrists and ankles, and the men fell heavily to the floor, sprawling across the bodies of other prisoners.

The long night began. Huddled in the filthy straw, they could barely move their hands to brush away the crawling creatures that crept up their legs and across their faces.

But thoughts of Jesus filled their minds. They knew that whatever happened, Jesus would take care of them. If they remained in prison, His Holy Spirit would be there to comfort them. Should they be killed, they would be resurrected on that day when Jesus returned to earth, and He would take them to live with Him in heaven.

And so they slept.

Early the next morning loud voices awakened them, and more guards hauled them before the Sanhedrin. Annas, the high priest, and Caiphas, his powerful son-in-law, stood ready to question them. But others, including Eliku, the healed begger, crowded into the room.

"By what power or what name did you do this?" Annas challenged the disciples.

Peter and John, filled with the Holy Spirit, were happy to answer. In a voice that all could hear, Peter proclaimed, "Rulers and elders of the people! If we are being called to account today for an act of kindness shown to a cripple and you demand to know how he was healed, then you and all the people of Israel must understand our explanation. It is by the name of Jesus Christ of Nazareth, whom you crucified but whom God raised from the dead, that this man stands before you healed.

"Salvation is found in no one else, for there is no other name under heaven given to human beings by which we must be saved."

The disciple's words shocked the high priest and other members of the Sanhedrin. Where did these unschooled fishermen find the courage to stand up to them like that? And how were they able to speak with such fluency, logic, and conviction? Their manner of speaking reminded them very much of Someone else who had spoken to them with supreme authority. And that Someone was Jesus Himself.

"What are we going to do?" they demanded of each other as they huddled together. "Everyone in Jerusalem knows they have performed a miracle—and we cannot deny it. But to stop this thing from spreading any further among the people, we must at least warn these men to speak no longer to anyone in the name of Jesus!"

Again they faced the prisoners. In their most grave and threatening tones they commanded, "From this day forward you are neither to speak nor teach in the name of Jesus!"

But Peter and John knew they could not obey that command. Their reply astonished the priests. "You be the judge. Should we obey you, or should we obey God? For we cannot help speaking about what we have seen and heard."

The high priest and members of the Sanhedrin huffed and blustered, shouting threats, muttering about what would happen to them if they persisted in following their dangerous course. They wanted to punish them right there and then. But how could they punish them for healing a man? And how could they ever get away with it when the crowds still sang praises for the miracle that Peter and John had performed through the power of the Holy Spirit?

As Peter and John walked across the sun-filled Temple courts, they knew they would spend the rest of their lives proclaiming the name of Jesus.

Where Shall We Meet for Worship?

Although church buildings and Christianity go together in most people's minds, Christians did not have their own buildings to meet together in for many centuries after the death of Christ.

The followers of Jesus who lived in Jerusalem continued to attend services in the Temple. Acts 2:46 tells how they "spent much time together in the temple" (NRSV). They assembled in the colonnaded buildings on the Temple Mount. Acts 5:12 mentions that they gathered in an area called Solomon's Portico.

Besides the Temple, Jerusalem's Christians came together in private homes, where they celebrated the Lord's Supper and perhaps shared a communal meal (Acts 2:46). They would also meet in homes for fellowship.

Elsewhere the followers of Jesus, still considering themselves Jews, went with their fellow Jews to the local synagogue each Sabbath. The book of Acts describes how as Paul and other evangelists went on their missionary trips, they would go to the synagogues in each town, hoping to convince the Jews and interested Gentiles who worshiped there to accept Jesus as their Messiah.

In time tensions and hostility between some of the Jewish leaders and the followers of Jesus forced the Christians to stop coming to the synagogues. The Jewish revolt and destruction of the Temple in Jerusalem brought an end to Christians meeting there. Christians began to gather only in private homes.

At first the Roman authorities would not allow Christians to construct their own meeting halls. They were afraid that when people gathered together for any reason, the group might be plotting revolt or insurrection. Christians had to make do with either house churches or meeting out in the open somewhere near the city. Wealthier members who had larger houses would provide space in their homes for believers to worship as a group.

House churches at first formed only in cities. The people in the country resisted the new religion of Christianity more strongly. In fact, the term *pagan* that Christians began to use for nonbelievers comes from the Latin word used to refer to peasants or country dwellers. The countryside was usually the last area in a region converted to Christianity.

The city of Rome had underground cemeteries called catacombs. Christians began to meet in them, especially during times of persecution.

As the numbers of Christians grew too big for house churches and the government became less hostile toward them, Christians began erecting buildings for worship. They patterned them after the Roman public buildings called basilicas. A basilica consisted of one main room called a nave with columns supporting the roof running along the side walls. A wooden clerestory roof with windows in it allowed air to circulate and light to enter. The building was oblong in shape with one end semicircular. Tribunals and public assemblies met in them.

Christians would put the altar at the semicircular end. A screen or low wall separated the altar from the congregation. Basilica churches had no seats or pews. The people would stand during the worship services. Even today Eastern Orthodox Christians stand during their two- to three-hour services.

When the Roman government recognized Christianity as the official state religion, it began giving Christians pagan temples and shrines to convert into churches. Christians also began modifying the basilica pattern into other architectural designs. House churches vanished for many centuries. They have reappeared in countries where the authorities will not permit certain groups of Christians to build their own places of worship.

⑥
Grand Opening

The December Sunday dawned bright and cold. Stacey opened her eyes and stared at the ceiling as she always did when morning touched her window and brushed her curtains with soft yellow light.

For a moment the girl didn't think about anything in particular. She just lay very still, soaking up the peaceful seconds like a dry sponge dipped in water. She felt tired, in a good sort of way—the kind of tired a person feels when they've worked hard and seen something beautiful rise from their labors.

Then she let her mind focus more clearly on the day ahead. A smile spread across her young face. This Sunday would be like no other Sunday in the history of Valley Springs—in her own history as well, for that matter.

On this day the Appleby-Brewster Museum of Antiquity would open wide its doors for the first time. On this day her beloved grandfather would stand before a thankful town and welcome them into his dream come true. And on this day he would receive a wonderful surprise, something Stacey had known about for a long time. The waiting would finally be over.

Slipping from her bed, she dropped to her knees, hands folded in front of her. "Thank You, Jesus," she prayed. "Thank You for this day and the wonderful things that are about to happen."

⚅ ⚅ ⚅

Professor Appleby stared at his reflection in the mirror. "Good morning, you crazy old man," he said with a grin. "What do you want to do today? Sit around and read? Clean up a bit? Perhaps write a letter to Maggie B?" He stepped back. "Or do you want to open a museum with the whole town of Valley Springs cheering you on?"

The professor frowned at his reflection. "Decisions, decisions." Stumbling to his bedroom, he stood in front of his open closet.

"What does one wear to a museum opening?" he asked. "Formal? Casual? Gardening?" Before him hung exactly three white shirts, three red sweaters, three pairs of slightly wrinkled pants, and a collection of bow ties, all of them green.

Then he glanced at his nightstand. There sat the little package Miss Baker had given to him on Friday, before he'd left the museum. "Don't open this until Sunday morning," the woman had warned. "It's something special for our special day."

The old man ambled over to his bed and sat down, bracing himself against the uneven tilt of his mattress. "And what have we here?" he asked playfully. "A new car? Perhaps my very own snowblower." He unwrapped the tiny parcel. "Nope, too little."

As he peered inside, his eyes opened wide. There, hiding in a soft bed of paper, sat a brand-new bow tie—bright blue in color.

"Blue?" the man gasped. "Blue? I've never worn a blue bow tie in all my—" He paused as a warm feeling crept into his heart. "I think my friend is trying to tell me something," he whispered to himself. "Dear ol' Anna's trying to tell me that maybe I should allow some changes into my life." He picked up the gift and studied it for a long time. Rising, he walked back to the bathroom and stood staring into the mirror. Slowly his hand came to rest at his throat, the new bow tie held firmly in his grip. "Looks pretty good," he said. "Yes, sir, it looks just fine."

Anna Baker lowered the phone receiver onto its cradle and smiled. Everything was now in place. All the details had been worked out. Her friend Professor Appleby would remember this day for the rest of his life.

She sniffed the air expectantly. Breakfast was almost ready. The warm, sweet smell of blueberry muffins baking in her oven filled her small apartment with a happy scent.

Miss Baker glanced at the photo resting on the kitchen table. It was a picture of her and Professor Appleby snapped many, many months ago out at his old Victorian mansion. They'd been working to establish the first museum there. The man's hair was sticking out in random fashion, his clothes covered with dust. But it was his smile that even now caught her eye. Such honesty. Such compassion. That same smile had taken her breath away the first day she'd seen him stumbling to the front door of his forest home.

A buzzer went off nearby. The muffins were done. Soon it would be time to dress and head to the campus. Miss Baker wasn't quite sure what she was looking forward to most—the grand opening of the new museum, or seeing, once again, the old professor's smile.

By the time 1:00 p.m. rolled around, the snow-carpeted lawn fronting the new history wing was packed with people, all eager to step into the ancient world offered by the long-awaited addition to the campus. Students and townspeople milled about, smiling, laughing, exchanging greetings, enjoying the bit of warmth generated by the bright sun overhead.

It seemed the entire community was on campus this day. Dignitaries, business owners, farmers, merchants, the very old, the very young, had all found their way to the college, prompted by the kind voice of Mr. McDonald on the radio and the repeated announcements printed by Mrs. Roth in the newspaper.

Stacey, Maria, and Jason couldn't stand still for a minute. They hurried about passing out information sheets to the press, greeting classmates from school, and whispering among themselves, always with one eye glued to the big clock hanging from the library tower.

As its long hands at last showed 1:00, the bells in the tower chimed loudly. On cue, Dr. Morrison's voice echoed across the frozen ground.

"Ladies and gentlemen of Valley Springs, as well as our guests," he spoke into the microphone perched on a long metal stand, "welcome to the grand opening of the new Appleby-Brewster Museum of Antiquity." Heads turned to see the college president positioned at the top of the steps leading to the museum entrance. Miss Baker was on his left, and Professor Appleby stood straight and tall at his right—a new blue tie resting just below his wrinkled neck. A yellow ribbon hung across the doorway, temporarily sealing the entrance.

"First I want to extend a warm Valley Springs welcome to each and everyone of you here today. As you know, this museum has been a long time in coming. Much sacrifice went into its construction. The chair of our History Department, Dr. Anna Baker, deserves a big round of applause." The crowd clapped their hands together enthusiastically as Miss Baker stepped forward. She bowed shyly and smiled down at the sea of faces. Lifting her hands she silenced the uproar.

"As much as I'd like to take all the credit for this new addition, I know I can't. Besides the good professor standing up here before you, there are three children who must be honored today. They've done more to make this a reality than everyone else combined. It was their enthusiasm, their ceaseless energy, their unflinching dedication to their friend Professor Appleby and his sister that changed minds, motivated hearts, and created the atmosphere needed to make all this happen." She turned and motioned behind her. Hesitantly Stacey, Maria, and Jason moved from the shadows of the building and stood awkwardly at the top of the steps. "I'd like to introduce you to Stacey Roth, Maria Rodriguez, and Jason Matthew Cartright—three of the finest, most hardworking citizens ever to come out of Valley Springs."

The roar from the crowd was almost deafening. The three children smiled bravely, although each looked as if they would rather be *anywhere* than standing by Miss Baker listening to a town show their appreciation.

As the tumult eased, Stacey stepped forward, her knees barely able to support her. "I want to say something," she announced into the microphone. The crowd hushed expectantly. She tried to speak, but no words would sound. Turning to Maria, the gathering heard her whisper, "I knew this would happen. I don't have any spit."

Maria raced down the steps and returned immediately with a handful of snow. Stacey tossed some into her mouth and swished it around. "There, that's better," she said.

Clearing her throat and drawing confidence from the many faces smiling up at her, she continued. "I just want to present my grandfather with a gift. We finished 'em on Friday." She turned and reached into her jacket pocket. When her hand reappeared, it was clutching a small parcel. Looking up at Professor Appleby, she said, "This is the first one. We saved it for you, Grandfather."

The old man took the package and eagerly unwrapped it. Inside he found a brand-new book with a title that caught his eye immediately. It read *Mysterious Stories From the Bible.*

"Oh," he breathed. "It's Maggie's book."

"Her first one," Stacey stated. "We printed it right here on campus. We're going to make others, you know. Six volumes in all. Dr. Morrison said we could."

"Oh," the old man repeated. "You wonderful children. You amazing, wonderful children. How can I ever thank you?"

Stacey grinned broadly. "Just be our friend for ever and ever. That's all the thanks we need."

"Is this my big surprise?" the man whispered, "the one you've all been giggling about?"

Stacey's grin broadened. "Maybe it is. Maybe it isn't."

Dr. Morrison stepped forward once again. "By the way, copies of this new exciting book will be on sale inside," he announced. "Please, everyone, buy *lots* of them. Our poor printing press is on its last leg. I think these kids wore it down completely."

The crowd laughed and nodded.

"And now," the college president continued, "it's time for the big event. I've asked our friend Professor Appleby to do the honors." Handing the old man a pair of oversized scissors, Dr. Morrison stepped back. The professor moved to the ribbon and paused, a nervous smile lighting his face. Clearing his throat, he looked down on the assembled throng. His hand trembled slightly as he spoke.

"My friends, this is a proud day for me. It's a dream come true." He hesitated as if searching for words. A hushed silence fell over the gathering, all eyes on the old man standing at the top of the stairs. "But it's not only my dream you fulfilled this fine afternoon. You see, I have a sister named Maggie B. She's the most precious person in the world to me. *She's* the one you honor most with your presence and this beautiful museum." Tears filled his eyes. "I haven't seen her for a very long time. She keeps herself sorta busy traveling around, writing stories and digging in the sands of distant places. But if she was here today—"

Professor Appleby's voice suddenly faltered. He stared into the crowd with an intensity that caused others to glance where he was looking. The old man blinked. There was a face among the many, a kind, loving face framed by snow-white hair, gazing back at him with clear, blue eyes. The smile was loving and proud, a smile he'd seen many times during his younger days.

The scissors slipped from his fingers and clattered to the ground. "Maggie," he whispered. "Maggie."

The old woman moved through the hushed gathering and made her way to the base of the steps. Looking up at the man, she spoke softly, tenderly. "I've come home, big brother," she said. "I've come home to stay."

A cheer rose from the crowd as Professor Appleby hurried down the steps and encircled his sister in his arms. He wept openly, his tears of joy mingling with those streaming down the face of the woman who, up until this moment, had been only a memory in his heart.

Miss Baker, trying to control her own emotions of happiness, picked up the scissors and lifted them high over her head. In a clear voice she called out, "On behalf of the community college, the citizens of Valley Springs, and two of the most loving, unselfish people I've ever known, I proclaim the Appleby-Brewster Museum of Antiquity officially open. Welcome, everyone. Welcome to a dream come true!"

With that she snipped the yellow ribbon. The crowd surged forward with shouts of anticipation.

At the base of the steps Professor Appleby and his sister Maggie B found themselves surrounded by the smiling faces and warm voices of a grateful town.

Stacey, Maria, and Jason stood nearby drinking in the unspeakable joy of the moment.

The promises and life-changing power contained in simple Bible stories had reached out from ancient lands and touched lives, just as they had for centuries, and just as they'll continue to do until the God who inspired them returns to take His children home.

WORD SEARCH—PERSONS

Find the hidden words in the puzzle below. They will read horizontally, vertically, or diagonally—frontward or backward. The names you need to find are listed below the puzzle grid. (Answers on page 119.)

```
L W T Y Z E D E K I A H H P T L Y C O Z
K Q W Q Y T I W G L D T S G Y C Z G M C
N I S I S E R A E D Z H N J K G N Y Z Y
H G X A C S V A E B A F Z S U S E J I S
A M Z I H W J G K B G Z C S A L O M E E
R O X N J K H I H U V G A O G T A G G D
O C C P H A I M E R E J P R W B Y S N G
B H C R P E T E R K E D E Z I H C L E M
E A T N E T Z Y V K X A U H S O J C J P
D V X I A H A X M O D N J N Z X W G K E
X E D T M C O X S A H P A I A C S D J R
D P D J Y Y G U U L Y A P C J C H T M M
M K E L I S A B E T H Q Y P C E T D T G
B H A Y O W D D M V I L Z L R N Y M N D
I S O I O N I K X K B N I O O M A I O C
N H A I R A H C E Z I K D S O N X A E I
F W Q F N F V L J Y Y I K D N R O R D P
L L Y A K N T G Y T A O I A V B Z A I D
U O W T I H U A U S L D H Y V D M S G G
J Y T J N X F D N H O J Y H C A Q M Q B
```

Anna	Herodias	Joshua	Sarai
Caiaphas	Jael	Lot	Sisera
Deborah	Jeremiah	Melchizedek	Zechariah
Elisabeth	Jesus	Peter	Zedekiah
Gideon	John	Salome	

Answer Key to Puzzles and Games

LOT'S ENEMIES (from page 24)

A m o r i t e s

ABC	MNO	MNO	PRS	GHI	TUV	DEF	PRS
2	6	6	7	4	8	3	7

K i n g   A d o n i Z e d e k

JKL	GHI	MNO	GHI	QZ	ABC	DEF	MNO	MNO	GHI	QZ	DEF	DEF	JKL
5	4	6	4	0	2	3	6	6	4	0	3	3	5

K i n g   o f   E g l o n

JKL	GHI	MNO	GHI	QZ	MNO	DEF	QZ	DEF	GHI	JKL	MNO	MNO
5	4	6	4	0	6	3	0	3	4	5	6	6

K i n g   o f   H e b r o n

JKL	GHI	MNO	GHI	QZ	MNO	DEF	QZ	GHI	DEF	ABC	PRS	MNO	MNO
5	4	6	4	0	6	3	0	4	3	2	7	6	6

K i n g   o f   J a p h i a

JKL	GHI	MNO	GHI	QZ	MNO	DEF	QZ	JKL	ABC	PRS	GHI	GHI	ABC
5	4	6	4	0	6	3	0	5	2	7	4	4	2

K i n g   o f   J a r m u t h

JKL	GHI	MNO	GHI	QZ	MNO	DEF	QZ	JKL	ABC	PRS	MNO	TUV	TUV	GHI
5	4	6	4	0	6	3	0	5	2	7	6	8	8	4

WHAT BALAK LEARNED (from page 38)

Prophetess	Deborah
Enemy leader	General Sisera
Tribe that helped send 10,000 men	Zebulun
Tools of war	Weapons
God's way to slow the chariots	Storm

God uses women too.

WELL, WELL, WELL (from page 66)

Jeremiah is imprisoned in well #7.

MYSTERY BABY (from page 82)

John the Baptist

WORD SEARCH—PLACES (from page 92)

```
L O Q A T D V G L U G P D P H H A W S C
O I L H G F K V W F F O T B G P U R L A
A E T Q A N F O R H B M M Q W H Y F B H
G G N L L Z A E T X N L K O H D N Q V C
N I E T R Q O E O E X J V G R A J G A E
U V Y B N T R R Y H D N N R C R L V F A
D N V R P A I Y B G C W Z O O S A D K N
C C W D Z N N A W L A I Y S K S A H Q K
R U H A G M I R L M B P R F Z H B D A S
G Q N B L P E D N E A H E E Z J M P I S
G J N F O U H G O L B E B D J S M H H O
Q D I I B W K P L A Y B W G F L A U P L
A X H U N R N M G S L R M H D E J R A Y
E T G J O E F L E U O O P E R L E U J Y
E V A C E T A O M R N N F T L J R V Q H
P C L P B J D U S E X D X U S A F P A L
B U I S I J Z Q V J Q I R R G U S X P O
U R L R G D K E Z Z K E G Y P T H T D F
L E E S K U P Z E F C X Z K B P R H U E
G X E A M O D O S A N J T E Q P K J V M
```

WORD SEARCH—PERSONS (from page 116)

```
L W T Y Z E D E K I A H H P T L Y C O Z
K Q W Q Y T I W G L D T S G Y C Z G M C
N I S I S E R A E D Z H N J K G N Y Z Y
H G X A C S V A E B A F Z S U S E J I S
A M Z I H W J G K B G Z C S A L O M E E
R O X N J K H I H U V G A O G T A G G D
O C C P H A I M E R E J P R W B Y S N G
B H C R P E T E R K E D E Z I H C L E M
E A T N E T Z Y V K X A U H S O J C J P
D V X I A H A X M O D N J N Z X W G K E
X E D T M C O X S A H P A I A C S D J R
D P D J Y Y G U U L Y A P C J C H T M M
M K E L I S A B E T H Q Y P C E T D T G
B H A Y O W D D M V I L Z L R N Y M N D
I S O I O N I K X K B N J O O M A I O C
N H A I R A H C E Z I K D S O N X A E I
F W Q F N F V L J Y Y I K D N R O R D P
L L Y A K N T G Y T A O I A V B Z A I D
U O W T I H U A U S L D H Y V D M S G G
J Y T J N X F D N H O J Y H C A Q M Q B
```